For the Sake of the World

CHURCH OF SWEDEN
Research Series

§

Göran Gunner, editor
Vulnerability, Churches, and HIV (2009)

Kajsa Ahlstrand and Göran Gunner, editors
Non-Muslims in Muslim Majority Societies (2009)

Jonas Ideström, editor
For the Sake of the World (2009)

For the Sake of the World
Swedish Ecclesiology in Dialogue with William T. Cavanaugh

Edited by
JONAS IDESTRÖM

☙PICKWICK *Publications* • Eugene, Oregon

FOR THE SAKE OF THE WORLD
Swedish Ecclesiology in Dialogue with William T. Cavanaugh

Church of Sweden, Research Series 3

Copyright © 2010 Trossamfundet Svenska kyrkan (Church of Sweden). All rights reserved. Except for brief quotations in critical publications or reviews, no part of this book may be reproduced in any manner without prior written permission from the publisher. Write: Permissions, Wipf and Stock, 199 W. 8th Ave., Suite 3, Eugene, OR 97401.

Pickwick Publications
An Imprint of Wipf and Stock Publishers
199 W. 8th Ave., Suite 3
Eugene, OR 97401

Scripture quotations are from New Revised Standard Version Bible, copyright © 1989 National Council of the Churches of Christ in the United States of America. Used by permission. All rights reserved.

www.wipfandstock.com

ISBN 13: 978-1-60899-108-2

Manufactured in the U.S.A.

Contents

Contributors

Introduction · JONAS IDESTRÖM 1
    Church in Sweden—a Brief Account
    Disposition
    Bibliography

Separation and Wholeness: Notes on the Unsettling Political Presence of the Body of Christ · WILLIAM T. CAVANAUGH 7
    The Sui Generis Political Form of the People of God
    Two Cities, Two Powers, Two Kingdoms
    The Church and Modern States
    Bibliography

Sacrament as Social Process: Some Historical Footnotes · ARNE RASMUSSON 32
    Baptism and the One Body of Christ
    Breaking Bread Together
    The Spirit's Freedom in the Meeting
    The Universality of Charisma
    Fraternal Admonition
    Conclusion
    Bibliography

Space, Materiality and the Politics of Leaving: Church of Sweden and Rosengård's Social Segregation · HENRIK WIDMARK 49
    Aftermath of a Society in Change
    The Act of Leaving
    Space
    The Building
    The Territorial Church
    Multiculturalism
    A Sense of Belonging
    Post Scriptum
    Bibliography

Contents

Social Agent—a Queer Role for the Church · NINNA EDGARDH 65
    Queer Perspectives
    Insult Turned on its Head
    For the Sake of the World
    Churches as Social Agents
    Functional Differentiation and Gender
    Gender Complementarity
    The Queer Contribution
    Back to the Future
    Bibliography

She Keeps Bothering Me: Human Rights and Suffering · GÖRAN GUNNER 86
    A Crime Against Humanity and the Identity of the Church
    Human Suffering and the Good Life
    Human Suffering and Human Rights
    On Human Rights and the State
    She Keeps Bothering Me
    Church Priorities and a Human Rights-language
    Overcoming the Public—Private Divide
    A People-Centered Responsibility
    A People-Centered Distributive Justice
    What About the "Judge"?
    Remember—She Is Bothering Me
    Bibliography

"People of Faith"—a Different Kind of Body Economy? · ANTJE JACKELÉN 106
    The Context: a View from Outside
    The Context: a View from Inside
    Ecclesiology and the Church as a Social body
    Consequences for Traditional Ecclesiologies? From Purity to Hybridity
    Conclusion
    Bibliography

The Return of the Body: Re-imagining the Ecclesiology of Church of Sweden · OLA SIGURDSON 125
    The New Visibility of Social Embodiment
    Church and/or State as Organic Wholes?
    Embodiment, Practices and Space
    The Politics of Practice
    Concluding Remarks
    Bibliography

Contributors

Dr. William T. Cavanaugh is Professor of Theology at the University of St. Thomas, Minnesota, USA.

Dr. Ninna Edgardh is Associate Professor of Ecclesiology at Uppsala University, Sweden.

Dr. Göran Gunner is Researcher at the Church of Sweden Research Unit and Associate Professor at Uppsala University, Sweden.

Dr. Jonas Ideström is Doctor in Ecclesiology and a Minister in Church of Sweden.

Dr. Antje Jackelén is Bishop of the Diocese of Lund, Church of Sweden. Between 2001 and 2007 she taught Systematic Theology and Religion & Science at the Lutheran School of Theology at Chicago, USA, and was director of the Zygon Center for Religion and Science.

Dr. Arne Rasmusson is Associate Professor of Theology and Ethics at the University of Umeå, Sweden.

Dr. Ola Sigurdson is Professor of Systematic Theology at the University of Gothenburg, Sweden, and also active as a cultural journalist.

Dr. Henrik Widmark is Senior Lecturer at the department of Art History at the University of Gotland, Sweden.

Introduction

JONAS IDESTRÖM

This is a book about the concrete identity of the church. The reflections do not start from agreement on a common ecclesiology but from a common interest in doing ecclesiology based on concrete manifestations of the church, and in an understanding of the church existing for the sake of the world. The crucial ecclesiological question is: How? How does the church exist for the sake of the world? That is a question based on how we understand church, theology and politics and their interrelationships. The questions and reflections in this book are formulated in a Swedish context (even though they are not all about the Swedish context) with its characteristic history and ecclesial discourse.

In a Nordic context there are historically close relationships between the nation and the church.[1] At times one could argue that the two in reality were one. Things have changed. Since the year 2000 the relationship between Church of Sweden and the State has been officially changed in a way that makes it clear that today they are viewed as two distinct social bodies. That is, of course, only one of numerous examples of how the church, step by step, over a long period of time has changed its role as social agent. The time when the local priest was part of local governance now seems far away. So things have changed.

On the other hand, the long history of close relationships between nation and church has become an integral part of both national and church identity in a fundamental way. As scholars have pointed out, it is not a pure coincidence that today we see strong welfare states in nations

---

1. Ryman, "Nordic Churches," 1–17.

with a history of strong national Lutheran folk churches.² "The notion of the European state church has leaked into the culture and discourse of the society of which it is part."³ So even though one can make a good case for stating that a country like Sweden today is one of the most secular countries in the world, that is not the whole picture; 79% of the population are still members of Church of Sweden and 70% of the infants born in Sweden are baptized. And although church and state are now more clearly separated, the split is not complete. Fundamental aspects of Church of Sweden's identity are for example still regulated by the Swedish parliament. In a Swedish context, national identity and church identity are still intertwined in a complex way.⁴

As Peter Berger argues, modernity, in its variety of manifestations, brings about pluralism, so also into Swedish society (even though one can argue that the process began later in the Nordic countries than in other parts of Europe)⁵. Pluralism transforms religion "both institutionally and in the consciousness of individuals"⁶ but it also transforms the social imagination of the nation and its citizens. In that church identity is bound up with national identity, it follows that fundamental changes in the process of creating and upholding a national Swedish identity—what it means to be a Swede—necessarily raises questions about church identity. So does the changing relationship between church and state.

The present situation then forces Church of Sweden to raise fundamental questions concerning its own identity. Questions that arise from a specific Swedish context but are of such a general character that they have a broader relevance. The situation raises questions concerning the role of theology in society today and the relationship between theology, politics and the church.

This book is a result of a need to try to understand the role and nature of the church in relation to these questions and challenges. The arguments in the articles were presented and discussed at a symposium organized by Church of Sweden Research unit and held at Sigtunastiftelsen in Sweden in September 2008. A majority of the theologians invited were in one

2. Lodberg and Ryman, "Church and Society," 101.
3. Berger et al., *Religious America*, 27.
4. Berger et al., *Religious America*, 25.
5. Lodberg and Ryman, "Church and Society," 99–101.
6. Berger et al., *Religious America*, 13.

way or another related to Church of Sweden, while others had relations to other denominations in Sweden. The purpose of the symposium was not to reach consensus but to stimulate creative and critical discussions concerning theology, politics and the identity of the church. Therefore the theologians that participated and presented papers were chosen so that a plurality of perspectives on these issues would be represented.

American theologian William T. Cavanaugh, who has made himself known as a distinct voice in the discussion of ecclesiology and politics, was invited as key-speaker. In books like *Torture and Eucharist*, *Theopolitical Imagination* and *Being Consumed*, Cavanaugh has provided examples of a form of concrete and constructive ecclesiology. From a theopolitical perspective he has described and analyzed actual manifestations of the church in relation to issues such as nationhood, torture and economics. It is this fundamental approach to ecclesiology that was the frame for the discussions at the symposium and the texts in this volume. The contributors were not asked to focus on Cavanaugh's theology as such but to reflect on the concrete manifestations of the church in line with his ecclesiological approach. One could therefore describe the theological reflections in this book as a form of concrete ecclesiology. That is, critical theological reflections on the way the church is manifested in social and historical contexts as a social body. By using concepts like *body*, *queer*, *human rights*, *practices*, *social process*, and *space* the manifestations of the concrete church are critically and constructively analyzed from a theological perspective.

Of course one needs to be aware of the differences between for example a Swedish and an American context when doing ecclesiology. As Cavanaugh argues in his article, ecclesiology is always contextual. But, as his argument also shows, it is both possible and fruitful to get different contexts on speaking terms with one another. That is why a Roman Catholic theologian from the US was asked to reflect on the Swedish context and why ecclesiological reflections that come out of a Swedish context should have relevance for theologians in other parts of the world.

Since ecclesiology is contextual and that some of the discussions in the articles presuppose the Swedish context, a short presentation of the current situation in Sweden and its history is needed.

CHURCH IN SWEDEN—A BRIEF ACCOUNT

The church has been present for a millennium in what today is defined as Sweden. Early on, the life of the church was inculturated into people's daily lives and close relationships were established between the rulers and the church. Reaching the kings and their earls was part of a missionary strategy.[7] Three main centres were established in the North that developed into church provinces which "claimed allegiance both to Rome and to the national kingdoms that were evolving slowly into states and nations."[8] And as Ryman concludes, the provinces gradually developed into national churches long before the reformation. "Church and politics were intermingled long before the sovereign kings laid their hands on the churches."[9] The local parishes were dependent on the support of freeholding farmers and eventually everyone had to belong to the church.

With the reformation in the 16th century, the king broke with the pope in Rome, as well as with the Danish king as the head of the Nordic union, and in doing so strengthened his own power. In keeping with the reformers' theological influence, Swedish was adopted as the language of the church. The Bible and hymnbooks were translated; a new, state-financed translation of the Bible was published as recently as 2000. The influence of the king in ecclesiastical matters led to strong ties between church and State that lasted for centuries. "Theology and politics walked hand in hand."[10] Lutheranism has helped to hold Nordic societies together. The hegemony of Lutheran Orthodoxy lasted until the end of the eighteenth century, when the old order was challenged by new ideas such as liberalism, tolerance, and socialism. They gave rise to new ecclesial traditions, such as Methodism and Baptist, and the advent of new associations eventually resulted in the establishment of free churches. This was just one concrete aspect of the emerging modern society in which the church lost more and more of its earlier public role. But it took time. Prior to 1951, a Swedish citizen could not leave Church of Sweden without joining some other denomination. The welfare state was built up in Sweden during the twentieth century and the country achieved rapid economic growth, especially in the decades following the Second World War.

7. Ryman, "Nordic Churches," 3.
8. Ryman, "Nordic Churches," 4.
9. Ryman, "Nordic Churches," 5.
10. Ryman, "Nordic Churches," 9.

As mentioned earlier, the formal relationship between Church of Sweden and the State was changed in 2000. Today, the work and organization of the nationwide Church of Sweden are regulated by decisions in the Church Synod, not the Swedish parliament. In that sense, Church of Sweden today is just one of several denominations in Sweden. In reality, however, Church of Sweden still has a unique role in the Swedish society. Its identity as an "evangelical-Lutheran, democratic folk church"[11] is still spelled out in Swedish law and the political parties are still involved in the Church's decision making bodies—at both a national and a local level.

DISPOSITION

The first six articles in this volume were presented as papers in progress at the symposium in Sigtuna. The final article, by Ola Sigurdson, was written after the symposium when the six articles were in their final form. Sigurdson was asked to relate the six articles to each other—to get them on speaking terms with one another. Could he find a common thread that ran through the articles? What conclusions could he draw concerning the concrete identity of the church, with a focus on Church of Sweden, and the task of doing ecclesiology, based on the arguments in the articles?

As Sigurdson concludes, there is a need for the church to keep re-imagining its own identity as it moves on through time and space. Hopefully this volume will stimulate further constructive, ecumenical and critical ecclesiological reflections that can contribute to such a quest so that the church can be true to its mission to exist for the sake of the world.

BIBLIOGRAPHY

Berger, Peter, et al. *Religious America, Secular Europe. A Theme and Variations*. Aldershot: Ashgate, 2008.
Kyrkoordning—med angränsande lagstiftning för Svenska kyrkan. Stockholm: Verbum, 1999.
Lodberg, Peter, and Björn Ryman. "Church and Society." In *Nordic Folk Churches. A Contemporary Church History*. Ryman, Björn et al., 99–121. Grand Rapids: Eerdmans, 2005.
Ryman, Björn. "Nordic Churches." In *Nordic Folk Churches. A Contemporary Church History*. Björn Ryman, et al., 1–17. Grand Rapids: Eerdmans, 2005.

---

11. Lag (1998:1591) om Svenska kyrkan, §1–2, see *Kyrkoordning*, 261.

Separation and Wholeness

Notes on the Unsettling Political Presence of the Body of Christ

WILLIAM T. CAVANAUGH

One cannot do ecclesiology in the abstract, free of context, but my particular ecclesiological context—Roman Catholicism in the United States—is very different from the context of Church of Sweden. We do, however, have in common the fact that both Roman Catholicism in the United States and Church of Sweden have a history of ambivalence about the separation of church and state. It was not until the Second Vatican Council vindicated the work of Yves Congar, John Courtney Murray, and others, that the separation of church and state was officially accepted by the Roman Catholic Church as something more than a necessary but regrettable accommodation to modern life in a liberal social order. As Philip Hamburger has demonstrated, until the middle of the twentieth century, separation of church and state in the United States was championed primarily by anti-Catholic Protestant nativists who opposed any sort of state aid for Catholic schools.[1] More broadly, however, separation of church and state was opposed in official Catholic circles because it seemingly threatened to relegate Catholicism and its aspiration to affect the wholeness of life to a small reservation of private life. Catholicism was not a "religion" but a way of life, a "culture" perhaps, that must be sustained institutionally. The fear was that Catholicism as a whole culture could not be sustained where political institutions were not grounded in Catholic principles.

---

1. See Hamburger, *Separation*.

It has been fascinating for me to watch from afar how Church of Sweden has dealt with the question of the separation of church and state. It seems that the separation of 2000 has been accepted by the majority of active members of the Church. And yet there remains a strong aspiration to wholeness. Church of Sweden is often considered a "folk church," and therefore meant to represent the spiritual dimension of Swedish life as a whole. What this means exactly is of course contested. But entailed in the claim to be a folk church is the idea that the church is not merely a "religion," a privatized set of beliefs, but also in some sense a "culture" that embraces the whole life of its members. How to accomplish this separated from a welfare state that has also aspired to embrace the wholeness of the lives of its citizens remains an interesting question.

In this essay I ponder, from a theological point of view, the relationship between the separation of church and state and the Christian aspiration to wholeness, both of which I think are good ideas, if understood properly. On the one hand, wholeness is written into the Nicene Creed that virtually all Christians profess: we believe in one church that is holy, apostolic, and also catholic. The term *katholikos* is derived from the Greek *kath' holou*, "according to the whole."[2] Although the meanings are varied, the term indicates not merely extension but concentration, the integration of all of life in one place into a coherent whole. According to Henri de Lubac, catholicity suggests

> the idea of an organic whole, of a cohesion, of a firm synthesis, of a reality which is not scattered but, on the contrary, turned toward a center which assures its unity, whatever the expanse in area or the internal differentiation might be.[3]

As Karl Barth says, catholicity is "all-embracing; it speaks of an identity, a continuity, a universality sovereignly asserting itself within all the diversities."[4]

On the other hand, however, there is a dynamic within Christian practice that tends toward separation and division within the social order. This is what Carl Schmitt referred to as the "typically Judeo-Christian

---

2. Dulles, *Catholicity of the Church*, 14.

3. de Lubac, *Motherhood of the Church*, 174.

4. Barth, *Kirchliche Dogmatik*, IV:1, 783, quoted in de Lubac, *Motherhood of the Church*, 174.

division of the original political unity,"[5] a split in which Schmitt found much to lament. Rather than bringing the civil and the spiritual power into one coherent whole, as the pagans had done, the church has tended to remain a somewhat alien body in any social order, either insisting on its independence from the civil authorities or contending for influence against the civil powers.

In this paper I will explore the theo-logic of this separation, and discuss how it is related to the church's aspiration for wholeness. I will begin by showing in what sense the scriptural witness supports Schmitt's contention that Christianity lends itself to political division. I will then briefly explore how in three figures—Augustine, Gelasius I, and Luther—the division of political unity evolved and was tamed. The third section explores the fate of the church in two modern types of regimes, liberalism and social democracy, and argues for the robust recovery of the church's political presence.

THE *SUI GENERIS* POLITICAL FORM OF THE PEOPLE OF GOD

The term "political theology" in the twentieth century was first given prominence by German jurist and political theorist Carl Schmitt in his famous 1922 book by that title. Schmitt's name has forever and rightly been tarred by his stint as favored jurist of the Third Reich before falling out of favor in 1936. But Carl Schmitt remains an interesting figure for political theology, because he understood the nature of ecclesio-political questions so clearly—though he came to conclusions that no Christian theologian ought to accept. Schmitt was troubled by the church's tendency to weaken the state by dividing it from within, something he judged was endemic to Christian social orders. The quote about the "typically Judeo-Christian division of the original political unity" is from Schmitt's book on Thomas Hobbes' image of the Leviathan. One of the primary reasons Schmitt was interested in Hobbes was that Hobbes thought the key political task was the restoration of the original pagan unity of civil and spiritual power over against the Christian splitting of that unity. "The struggle to overcome the Roman papal church's division between a 'Kingdom of Light' and a 'Kingdom of Darkness'—that is, the restoration of the original

---

5. Schmitt, *Leviathan in the State Theory*, 10.

unity—is, as Leo Strauss ascertained, the actual meaning of Hobbes' political theory."[6] According to Strauss, Hobbes blamed the "revolutionary state-destroying distinction between religion and politics" on the Jews, but Schmitt argues that Hobbes' real concern was the Christian church, especially the pope and "power-thirsty Presbyterian churches."[7] The problem became acute in the medieval period with claims by the church to power in temporal matters, as in papal claims to be able to depose kings and emperors for the sake of spiritual goods, or in claims by the church to decide when a war is just and when it is not.[8] By the sixteenth century, the church, through Cardinal Robert Bellarmine, was still claiming an "indirect power" over temporal rulers, a claim that Hobbes directly and vehemently opposed.[9] Political authority was always split by the presence of the body of Christ. The Leviathan that Hobbes pictured—the state-body enacted by the will and right of each individual—would constantly have to struggle against this other body. As Schmitt says of the Leviathan, "For every good Christian it became a dread-provoking image to see a great animal juxtaposed to the *Corpus mysticum* of the man-god, the great Christ."[10]

According to Schmitt, the reason that the state was entitled to the undivided political obedience of the individual was that the state offered protection through its monopoly on the means of violence. Indirect powers such as the church were deceptive because they laid claim to obedience without providing protection in return. As Schmitt says, they enjoy all of the advantages and take on none of the risks that the possession of political power entails.[11] This division is deadly for the state, for "The wonderful armature of a modern state organization requires uniformity

---

6. Schmitt, *Leviathan in the State Theory*, 10.

7. Schmitt, *Leviathan in the State Theory*, 10.

8. Schmitt, *Leviathan in the State Theory*, 71.

9. Hobbes refutes Bellarmine's book *De Summo Pontifice* at length in Hobbes, *Leviathan* (chapter 42), 399–423.

10. Schmitt, *Leviathan in the State Theory*, 62.

11. Schmitt, *Leviathan in the State Theory*, 72–74. Schmitt writes, "If protection ceases, the state too ceases, and every obligation to obey ceases. The individual then wins back his 'natural' freedom. The 'relation between protection and obedience' is the cardinal point of Hobbes' construction of state. It permits a very good reconciliation with the concepts and ideals of the bourgeois constitutional state," 72.

of will and uniformity of spirit."[12] The great Leviathan needed to be able to act as a unified corporate person, with one will and spirit.

We will return to Schmitt's solution to this problem, and its relevance to the Swedish context, later. What is interesting for our purposes now is Schmitt's diagnosis of the inherently divisive nature of the church in the political realm and the importance Schmitt placed on taming that source of division. Schmitt saw clearly as few others have what is at stake in political theology: the contest of Leviathan and the *corpus mysticum* of the God-man, the state-body and the body of Christ. For Schmitt, the problem of an indigestible "indirect power" in the state-body cannot be resolved until the church gives up its pretensions to embody the same kind of political decision-making that belongs properly to the state alone. He thought it poisonous, for example, that the church could claim the right to decide what is or is not a just war. Schmitt thought the question of "Who decides?" was the key question. As he writes in his key text *Political Theology*, abstract talk about the superiority of the spiritual power to the temporal power is meaningless, because (he quotes Hobbes), "Subjection, Command, Right, and Power are accidents not of Powers but of Persons."[13] Political decision-making is embodied not in law but in the person of the state sovereign, who cannot share such decision-making with another body.

Schmitt was exactly right to see that the splitting of the original political-spiritual unity of pagan culture is a fundamental and typical aspect of Christian belief and practice. From a Christian point of view, Schmitt was wrong to try to tame it. The splitting of political order is just the expression of the idea that salvation has a history. The appearance of a chosen people and a Messiah in time—and the continuation of time after the appearance of the Messiah but before the full consummation of his reign—divides creation into two ways of representing rule: acceptance of the sovereignty of Christ over history, and failure to accept Christ's sovereignty as yet. This does not mean that those who fail to acknowledge Christ explicitly are precluded from some participation in Christ. But beginning with Abraham, the scandal of particularity becomes unavoidable: God decisively acts in history to separate out one particular people from creation as a whole, not because of the virtues of that people—their vices

---

12. Schmitt, *Leviathan in the State Theory*, 74.
13. Schmitt, *Political Theology*, 33–34.

are more often on display in the Old Testament—but because they are to help make visible to the world, for the sake of the world, the way that God would and does rule. All the nations of the world are to be blessed (Gen. 12:3), but through this peculiar people.

The call is not, by any means, "religious" as opposed to "political." As Walter Brueggemann says, "Israel's self-presentation is inescapably a *political theology* in which YHWH, the God of Israel, is intensely engaged with questions of power and with policies and practices that variously concern the distribution of goods and access."[14] The Law given to Israel is not divided into religious and political law; it covers the whole of Israelite life from interest on loans to the tassels on one's cloak. Where the splitting of political unity occurs is in the ambivalence of the scriptural texts with regard to how God's rule is represented on earth. The intimacy of God and king in some texts (e.g. 2 Sam 7:8–17) is juxtaposed with other texts in which the human king is seen as a usurper of God's kingship. When the elders of Israel ask Samuel for "a king to govern us, like other nations" (1 Sam 8:5), the LORD responds that "they have rejected me from being king over them" (1 Sam 8:7).[15] Thus the psalms that proclaim that the LORD is king (e.g. Pss 93, 95, 96, 97, 99) can be used either to exalt or to delegitimate human kingship. This ambivalence is not an accidental feature of the Old Testament, evidence of some mundane power struggles between pro- and anti-monarchical factions. Ambivalence about human sovereignty is a direct result of the intervention of God's rule in human history before the eschaton.

Even more important than ambivalence about the kings that Israel had is the fact that the unity of kingship and priesthood is a relatively brief period in the history of Israel. As scripture scholar Gerhard Lohfink argues, there is no reason to consider the relatively brief period of monarchy to be definitive of the social form of the people of God. For the two hundred years before David, the Israelites chose to remain a loose tribal confederation, not because they were incapable of imitating their neighbors, but as a deliberate counter-model to Babylonian and Egyptian

14. Brueggemann, "Old Testament," 9.

15. Similar texts include Judges 9:7–15—in which Jotham's parable has the productive trees refuse to become king over the other trees, until the useless bramble agrees to reign—and 1Kings 12:1–19—in which King Rehoboam's deliberate cruelty is highlighted. The passage in First Kings concludes, "So Israel has been in rebellion against the house of David to this day."

models of monarchy in which a sacral kingship was part of the order of creation. To be "like other nations" was not considered something to which to aspire. The equality and free association of the tribal model were valued by the Israelites, largely because they saw themselves as equally under the rule of God.[16] The later critiques of monarchy can only be understood in light of this tradition in Israelite thinking and practice.

The period of monarchy lasted until the fall of the northern kingdom to the Assyrians in 722BC and the fall of the southern kingdom to the Babylonians in 587BC. In the meantime, the people of God were introduced to forced labor, wars of territorial conquest, and the development of pronounced class-based inequality. There was, for the first time, a union of throne and altar, and YHWH became a kind of official "state god." The later review of this period in the deuteronomistic history was mixed, but was on the whole quite critical. The deuteronomistic history does not regard this period as without purpose. The way had been prepared for the later advent of a successor of David who would rule as a direct instrument of God's sovereignty.[17] It would be a mistake, however, to infer that the Davidic monarchy was therefore paradigmatic of the social form of the people of God. To the contrary, as Oliver O'Donovan says, it is the Babylonian Exile that becomes the paradigm of Jewish existence.[18]

After the relatively brief period of the unity of throne and altar, the people of God existed as a sub-society within the larger framework of the imperial powers that dominated them. Under the Babylonians, Persians, Ptolemys, and Seleucids, Israel had limited autonomy and self-government, existing as a foreign body within the larger empire-body. There was no Israelite king, but life revolved around the Temple, and the high priest took on roles that a modern person would consider "political," attending to matters of organization, taxation, and law. Political unity in the empire, in other words, was divided by the distinctiveness of the people of God. Their identity in this period was cemented by the Torah, which, as Lohfink notes, is based in the pre-Davidic stories of creation and liberation and excludes only the Israelite experience as a territorial monarchy. Lohfink believes this omission was deliberate, a statement that Israel's essential character is established not under David and Solomon, but instead

---

16. Lohfink, *Does God Need the Church?*, 107–9.
17. Lohfink, *Does God Need the Church?*, 109–12.
18. O'Donovan, *Desire of the Nations*, 83.

in the memory of a "priestly kingdom and holy nation" (Ex 19:6) liberated from slavery and living under God's direct rule. Sinai is neither Egypt nor Jerusalem. The priestly kingdom is not a sacral monarchy, for the priestly function mediates God's kingship directly to the people, bypassing earthly monarchs. In the priestly kingdom, there was to be no oppression, and the poor and the weak were to be taken care of. God was to be the sole ruler of Israel, in every aspect of life, and God's law was to maintain the identity of the people of God under whatever earthly regime appeared to rule.[19] The point was not simply to maintain the identity of Israel, however. The people of God existed for the sake of the world. The echo of Genesis 12:3 can be heard in Jeremiah 29:7: "seek the welfare of the city where I have sent you into exile, and pray to the LORD on its behalf, for in its welfare you will find your welfare."

The typical Judeo-Christian division of political unity in this period took the form of a non-sovereign, non-territorial priestly social body that obeyed a different ruler within the framework of a foreign political rule. This social form continued as the people of God became a federation of synagogues in the Diaspora. The synagogue was more than a place of worship; it was also a place for judicial assemblies, business transactions, receiving travelers, feeding the poor, and mourning the dead. The federation of synagogues was not a *polis*, but neither was it merely a *koinon* or *thiasos*, a semi-private club gathered around a particular interest. The synagogue was concerned with the whole of life, every detail of which was covered by the Torah. This very concern for wholeness is precisely the reason that the Jews fit awkwardly into Roman society. They were allowed exemption from military service and later from the official imperial cult, in deference to the "customs of their ancestors."[20]

As long as Christians were considered Jews, these exemptions applied to them as well. As Lohfink remarks:

> It is important for us to note that the association of communities discovered by Israel became the formative principle of the early church. Here appeared with full clarity what the people of God is: a network of communities spread over the whole earth and yet existing within non-Christian society, so that each person can freely choose whether to be a Christian or not; it is genuine com-

---

19. Lohfink, *Does God Need the Church?*, 112–14.
20. Lohfink, *Does God Need the Church?*, 117–18.

munity and yet not constructed on the model of pagan society, a true homeland and yet not a state.[21]

The early Christians borrowed the term *ekklesia* for the church, a political term that for the Greeks referred to the gathering of those with citizen rights in a given *polis*. The church thus signaled that it was not a private club, but a public entity with an interest in the whole of life.[22] Wholeness, again, is what produces the splitting of political unity: in the midst of the empire there exists a community whose claim to rule is just as comprehensive as that of Caesar. The Christian is to put her whole way of life under the rule of God. Precisely because there is no separation of religion and politics, there must be separation of church and state.

The Gospel episode of Caesar coin (Mt 22:15–22) is therefore not to be understood in modern terms as a placid division of labor between God and Caesar. The inscription on the denarius used to pay the temple tax read "Tiberius Caesar, son of the divine Augustus, great high priest."[23] Between this emperor who claimed to be the son of a god, and the Jesus of whom his followers made the same claim, there could be no easy settlement. Jesus would have been familiar with the opening of Psalm 24 and its trenchant claim to wholeness: "The earth is the LORD's, and all that is in it" (Ps 24:1). If we give to God what is God's—everything—there would be nothing left for Caesar.

The claim that Jesus was the son of God had clear echoes in 1 Samuel 7:14, and served to link Jesus to the claim of Davidic kingship. David remained normative for messianic thought; messianic expectations among Jews tended to focus on a descendent of David who would come and restore the territorial kingdom of Israel through military might. That Jesus effected no such restoration, and in fact ended up on a cross, was interpreted by the early church as a sign not that Jesus had abandoned all pretensions to rule, but that he had redefined rule in the light of the cross and resurrection. The "messianic secret" motif in Mark works to deny the expectations of a messianic king who comes in glory. Jesus refuses to accept the title "Messiah" in public (Mk 8:27–38) until he is the captive of the powers, being led to his death (Mk 14:62). In the book of Revelation, it is the slaughtered Lamb who rules (Rev 5:11–14). The cross is not the

---

21. Lohfink, *Does God Need the Church?*, 118.
22. Lohfink, *Does God Need the Church?*, 218–19.
23. See Brown, *New Jerome Biblical Commentary*, 665.

postponement of the Kingdom of God, its deferral until some later time when Jesus comes back and finally gets it right. The cross *is* the coming of the Kingdom, the inauguration of the reign of self-sacrificial love.[24]

What is decisive ecclesiologically and politically is that the church believed that it was participating in the Lamb's rule. The saints sing:"You are worthy to take the scroll and to open its seals, for you were slaughtered and by your blood you ransomed for God saints from every tribe and language and people and nation; you have made them to be a kingdom and priests serving our God, and they will reign on earth" (Rev 5:9-10). The church of the book of Revelation did not believe it would assume Caesar's power and rule like Domitian did, nor that the coming of God's reign was deferred until some decisive future coming of Christ, wielding the same kind of power that Caesar wielded. Unlike Leviathan, Christ does not offer protection in return for obedience; for Schmitt, this is precisely why the body of Christ cannot be properly political. As John Howard Yoder comments on this passage of Revelation, however, the church's statement about the slaughtered Lamb was a political statement about the way the world is really governed; despite appearances, the world is not really controlled by the kings and emperors of this world, but by the God who is embodied in the Crucified One.[25] The Christian division of political unity is between the way the world appears to be run and the way it really is. The political task of the church is to witness to the way that Christ rules, through servanthood that does not look much like sovereignty in the world's eyes. The church is meant to make visible to the world what the justice of God looks like. The church claims to be nothing less than the visible body of the slaughtered Lamb. "God put this power to work in Christ when he raised him from the dead and seated him at his right hand in the heavenly places, far above all rule and authority and power and dominion, and above every name that is named, not only in this age but also in the age to come. And he has put all things under his feet and has made him the head over all things for the church, which is his body, the fullness of him who fills all in all" (Eph 1:20–23). This claim by the church to be the "fullness of him who fills all in all" should not be an arrogant claim to power, for the Christ that the church is to make visible to the world is the slaughtered Lamb, whose rule does not resemble Leviathan's.

24. Yoder, *Politics of Jesus*, 60–61.
25. Yoder, "To Serve Our God and to Rule the World," 130–35.

Because the church is the body of Christ, authority in the church is sacramental; this is a point that Yoder fails to fully appreciate. The Eucharist makes the church, as Henri de Lubac famously put it. This means that priestly authority is decisive in the body of Christ. Christ joins the offices of priest, prophet, and king, but the priestly office—in which the laity shares—is that which sacramentally constitutes the body of Christ. Earthly priesthood can never be absorbed by earthly kingship because earthly priesthood directly mediates the divine presence as earthly kingship cannot. Any direct royal claim of divine sanction that is not mediated by the church stumbles on the power of the Eucharist. The Eucharist, furthermore, is the foretaste on earth of the eternal rule of God, the eschatological consummation of the Kingdom of God, the banquet of the slaughtered Lamb.[26] The slaughtered Lamb, however, does not offer protection in exchange for obedience, not in Hobbes' sense anyway; the Lamb offers the crown of martyrdom.

TWO CITIES, TWO POWERS, TWO KINGDOMS

The typical Judeo-Christian splitting of political unity would take a detour with Constantine's efforts to act as a universal bishop over the church. A blanket condemnation of "Constantinianism" as the decisive fall of the church is not very helpful, however. In the first place, such a condemnation does not take account of the movement of the Holy Spirit in history, and the possibility that God will write straight with crooked lines. If we are not to assume that the church simply went into wholesale apostasy following Constantine's conversion, then we must see the experiment with Christian emperors as an attempt to bring the Gospel to the wholeness of life. In the second place, a blanket condemnation of Constantinianism fails to appreciate the continued efforts in the medieval period to maintain the typically Christian division of political unity.

Augustine's image of two cities—the *civitas terrena* and the *civitas Dei*—preserves in a significant way the eschatological tension between the reign of God and earthly political rule. Augustine's image of two cities assumes the paradigmatic nature of the Babylonian Exile; the experience of the *civitas Dei* in its earthly pilgrimage is that of the People of God in

---

26. On the importance of the Eucharist as foretaste of the Kingdom of God for the early church, see Wainwright, *Eucharist and Eschatology*.

Babylon.²⁷ The two cities do not correspond to sacred/secular, private/public, or church/state dichotomies. There is no division of labor between things that are Caesar's and things that are God's. The two cities use the same temporal goods, but in different ways and for different ends.²⁸ The two cities, therefore, are not two different spaces but two different sets of practices that correspond to two different times, the *already* and the *not yet* of the Kingdom of God. All belongs to God; Christ has already definitively triumphed and the earthly city with its *libido dominandi* is passing away. The city of God recognizes that triumph. Resistance remains, and the Kingdom is not yet fully realized, but the *not yet* of the Kingdom has no ontological status. Although Augustine admitted the possibility and necessity of Christian participation in temporal government, the temporal was only a temporary necessity for the restraint of vice by vice. It had no status in nature, but was passing away before the triumph of Christ over the powers. The Roman republic and empire, says Augustine, had failed to be a true *res publica*.²⁹ It is the city of God that is the true public, and the actual performance of the city of God in time is Israel and the church.³⁰

According to Augustine, "two cities were created by two kinds of love: the earthly city was created by self-love reaching the point of contempt for God, the Heavenly City by the love of God carried as far as contempt of self."³¹ By the end of the fifth century, however, Pope Gelasius I would write "Two there are . . . by which this world is ruled,"³² a dictum that would come to be deeply influential in the medieval period. Rather than two distinct cities, there was now one city with two powers, priesthood and kingship. Rather than two ways of dealing with temporal goods, one acknowledging Christ's rule and the other seeking its own glory, there was now one city divided into two spheres of influence, and, as Gelasius

---

27. Augustine, *City of God*, XIX, 26.
28. Augustine, *City of God*, XVIII, 54.
29. Augustine, *City of God*, XIX, 21–25.

30. Although Augustine distinguishes between the visible and invisible churches, the chaff and the wheat, he does say that the city of God is the church in XVI, 2, and says in XX, 9 that "the Church even now is the kingdom of Christ and the kingdom of heaven" because it contains the righteous within it.

31. Augustine, *City of God*, XIV, 28.
32. Gelasius I, "Letter to Emperor Anastasius," 179.

says, "each sphere has a specially qualified and trained profession."[33] The result of this division of labor was a more or less constant struggle for dominance between the civil and ecclesiastical powers during the medieval period. Ecclesiastical authorities claimed at least an indirect power and often a direct power over the civil authorities—the authority to name and depose rulers, especially—and their own system of courts. At the same time, the eschatological reference became muted, and the temporal power became a constant and natural feature of earthly life, rather than a temporary, stop-gap measure until the reign of Christ was fully realized.

The rise of sovereign territorial states largely put an end to the battles between civil and ecclesiastical power in many European countries, through the absorption of church power by the newly centralizing state. In the late fifteenth century, the civil authorities in England, Sweden, Denmark, and Germany tried—with only partial success—to limit clerical exemptions from civil courts, limit the power of ecclesiastical courts, and transfer church appointments, revenues, and lands to the civil rulers. As Quentin Skinner points out, the Reformation failed in France and Spain, where the monarchies had largely absorbed the church into their clientage systems, and therefore had an interest in maintaining the status quo.[34] As Pope Julius III wrote to Henry II of France, "in the end, you are more than Pope in your kingdoms . . . I know no reason why you should wish to become schismatic."[35] Where the Reformation succeeded was in England, Scandinavia, and many German principalities, where breaking with the Catholic Church meant that the church could be used to augment the power of the civil authorities. To cite one example, King Gustav Vasa welcomed the Reformation to Sweden in 1524 by transferring the receipt of tithes from the church to the crown. Three years later he appropriated the entire property of the church.[36]

Martin Luther theorized this shift by denying that temporal and spiritual formed two bodies. To say so, as Luther wrote to the Christian nobility in Germany, was in effect to say that Christ himself has two bodies.[37] Christ has only one body, with a division of labor within it that

---

33. Gelasius I, "The Bond of Anathema," 178–79.
34. Skinner, *Foundations of Modern Political Thought*, 2:58–64.
35. Pope Julius III, quoted in Potter, *History of France*, 227.
36. Skinner, *Foundations of Modern Political Thought*, 2:60–61.
37. Luther, "To the Christian Nobility of the German Nation," 14–15.

corresponds to a division between temporal and spiritual, or external and internal, matters. Luther thereby denies that the church can have any legitimate power over temporal matters, or that the church as a body could split the original political unity. At the same time, the temporal power has direct jurisdiction over the church in temporal matters, and ecclesiastical courts are abolished.[38]

Luther's division between the two kingdoms is not a division between two bodies politic, but a division of labor that runs not only within each polity but through each individual. There exist two kingdoms or governments: one spiritual, by which the Holy Spirit produces true Christians, and the other temporal, by which the un-Christian are restrained and order is kept. "Both must be permitted to remain; the one to produce righteousness, the other to bring about external peace and prevent evil deeds. Neither one is sufficient in the world without the other."[39] Augustine's eschatological horizon has been removed; the temporal is a permanent feature of life on earth. Temporal government is necessary "for the world and the masses are and always will be un-Christian, even if they are baptized and Christian in name."[40] The eschaton is thus indefinitely deferred. The split between the *already* and the *not yet* of the Kingdom of God is therefore not a political split, but a split that runs through every individual Christian. The typical Christian splitting of political unity has become a split between a Christian's obedience to the Sermon on the Mount and his or her responsibility to the state. True Christians should turn the other cheek amongst themselves, but they must be willing to serve the state as soldiers and hangmen to ensure that external order will reign in the world. As Luther writes, "at one and the same time you satisfy God's kingdom inwardly and the kingdom of the world outwardly. You suffer evil and injustice, and yet at the same time you punish evil and injustice."[41] Luther's distinction between inward and outward would be used eventually to support the privatization of religion as belief in liberal social orders.

---

38. Luther, "To the Christian Nobility of the German Nation," 15–16.
39. Luther, "Temporal Authority," 92.
40. Luther, "Temporal Authority," 91.
41. Luther, "Temporal Authority," 96.

THE CHURCH AND MODERN STATES

Carl Schmitt thought that the union of crown and altar in the early modern period brought only a temporary respite to the struggle of the state against indirect powers. According to Schmitt, the kind of distinction between inward and outward that Luther introduced led to the eventual dissolution of political unity.[42] For Luther, the state was God-ordained but remained essentially negative, a protective barrier to allow room for the real life of the Gospel. For Schmitt, this was insufficient.

> But when public power wants to be only public, when state and confession drive inner belief into the private domain, then the soul of a people betakes itself on the 'secret road' that leads inward ... At precisely the moment when the distinction between the inner and outer is recognized, the superiority of the inner over the outer and thereby that of the private over the public is resolved. Public power and force may be ever so completely and emphatically recognized and ever so loyally respected, but only as a public and only an external power, it is hollow and already dead from within. Such an earthly god has only the appearance and the *simulacra* of divinity on his side.[43]

The division of labor between inward and outward, soul and body, is unworkable according to Schmitt, not because the church should resist loss of political relevance, but because the state must not and cannot surrender divinity to an interiorized faith. The state god is a jealous god, and it cannot remain contented with only the body; it must have the soul as well.

According to Schmitt, since the nineteenth century the modern liberal state has institutionalized the split between inward and outward, private and public, society and state, thus marking a resurgence of the indirect powers that the absolutist state had quelled. "The old adversaries, the 'indirect' powers of the church and of interest groups, reappeared in

---

42. Although Luther is mentioned as one of those who introduce the inner/outer distinction, Schmitt concentrates on Hobbes' distinction between inner faith and outer conviction; the individual was entitled to preserve in his or her heart a private judgment contrary to the state's public confession. In this public/private distinction, Schmitt saw the seeds of the Leviathan's future destruction. Later thinkers like Spinoza would take Hobbes' private freedom of thought and make it into the form-giving principle of the state; Schmitt, *Leviathan in the State Theory*, 57–59; 62.

43. Schmitt, *Leviathan in the State Theory*, 61.

that century as modern political parties, trade unions, social organizations, in a word as 'forces of society.'"[44] The state had become nothing more than a legal framework for the exterior regulation of society. The state in liberalism became a forum for contending interests among the forces of society.[45] Where the theological image of the state has survived in liberalism, it is only as an immanent god: democracy identified the ruler and the ruled.[46] Schmitt cites Tocqueville's observation that, in American democracy "the people hover above the entire political life of the state, just as God does above the world, as the cause and end of all things."[47] This immanent god, however, bears only the simulacra of divinity.

In American-style liberalism, the immanent god of democracy has largely replaced the personal and transcendent element of sovereignty that Schmitt sought to rescue. Belief in a transcendent God is common in the United States, but liberalism aspires to separate that belief from the political life of the state, because sovereignty is derived from popular representation, and not from transcendent authority. American civil religion still invokes a vague "God," but it is not the God of Jesus Christ. The god of American civil religion corresponds to what Durkheim says of religion: it is the divinization of an immanent social process. The church, meanwhile, continues to worship the God of Jesus Christ, but the inward/outward distinction has become a separation of "religion" from "politics." The church has not only come to accept the separation of church and state, but has also learned to separate "religion" from "politics," such that Christians do not tend to see the body of Christ as representing the political sovereignty of God. The body of Christ is rather seen as a "religious" body, and the political life of individual Christians is represented through the platforms of the political parties. The body of Christ does not compete for space with the state-body. The church opines on public matters, such as the question of what is a just war and what is not, but the crucial matter of decision is left to the state.

Liberalism has not been the only way of resolving the Christian splitting of political unity in the twentieth century. The so-called "conservative revolution" associated with Schmitt and others has sought a more

---

44. Schmitt, *Leviathan in the State Theory*, 73.
45. Schmitt, *Leviathan in the State Theory*, 73–74.
46. Schmitt, *Political Theology*, 49–50.
47. Schmitt, *Political Theology*, 49.

robustly theological version of the state, with pernicious effects for the church. According to Schmitt:

> All significant concepts of the modern theory of the state are secularized theological concepts not only because of their historical development—in which they were transferred from theology to the theory of the state, whereby, for example, the omnipotent God became the omnipotent lawgiver—but also because of their systematic structure, the recognition of which is necessary for a sociological consideration of these concepts. The exception in jurisprudence is analogous to the miracle in theology.[48]

Only by recognizing this truth, thought Schmitt, can state sovereignty be put on a properly theological basis, and political authority take on more than just the simulacra of divinity. Only in this way could the inward/outward, private/public split be healed, and a unity of will and spirit be achieved in a decisive and personal sovereign. The church is to be rigidly excluded from the realm of the political; the church does not mediate between God and the state, but the state has direct access to divinity. Nevertheless, Christianity is not to be simply privatized. Schmitt was a Roman Catholic, and his early work *Roman Catholicism and Political Form* gave the church an essential legitimating function for the political, based on the church's "absolute realization of authority."[49] However, fellow German Catholics such as Erik Peterson regarded Schmitt's later work as abandoning the true public character of the Gospel in deference to the unity of the state. With Schmitt's appropriation of Hobbes, he saw authority as not preceding the state, but as a creation of the state. "Because state power is supreme, it possesses divine character. But its omnipotence is not at all divinely derived: It is a product of human work and comes about because of a 'covenant' entered into by man."[50] Divinity, in other words, is a characteristic of the state itself, and not a quality conferred by the same God the church serves. As Michael Hollerich notes, Schmitt's comments on Hobbes seem to apply to Schmitt himself: "Hobbes' displacement of Christianity into marginal domains was accomplished with the intent of rendering harmless the effect of Christ in the social and political sphere;

---

48. Schmitt, *Political Theology*, 36.
49. Schmitt, *Roman Catholicism*, 18.
50. Schmitt, *Leviathan in the State Theory*, 33.

of de-anarchizing Christianity, while leaving it in the background a certain legitimating function."[51]

The interpretation of Schmitt's Catholicism is a matter of controversy[52]; at any rate, I am not interested in Schmitt as such, but only insofar as he lays out the alternatives for a theology of the political so clearly. Schmitt interests me as well because the Swedish "Folkhemmet" of the mid-twentieth century has certain affinities with Schmitt's anti-liberalism. In social democracy in Sweden, resistance to the disintegrative effects of liberalism resulted in a strongly organic view of the social order and a personalization of state sovereignty. Indeed, the Leviathan appears in a different form in the work of Rudolf Kjellén, one of the architects of Swedish social democracy and a figure whom Ola Tunander calls "perhaps the most influential Scandinavian political scientist ever."[53] In Kjellén we find a concern to counter a flaccid liberal individualism and legalism with a view of the state as a "living organism." The state was not a minimal legal framework meant to keep order, but was the expression of the whole life of a people. As Tunander puts it, Kjellén's "organic view of the state was an attempt to regard the state as an independent object of study with its own dynamic and logic, power and will, an organic unity of land and people, an organism with body and soul, a personality on the international stage."[54] Kjellén analyzed the way that people spoke of corporate entities like "Germany" and "England" acting, judging, fighting, parenting, and so on. He thought it most realistic to speak of the state not merely as a legal framework, but as a corporate body—Mother Sweden or Uncle Sam—striding across the international stage. The state-body was an organic unity of land and people, a combination of geo-politics and ethno-politics. In this sense, nation-states were natural, and land and people had a shaping influence on the "cultural" side of the state, its gov-

---

51. Hollerich, "Carl Schmitt." The internal quote is from Barbara Nichtweiß's study of Erik Peterson.

52. Heinrich Meier's *The Lesson of Carl Schmitt: Four Chapters on the Distinction between Political Theology and Political Philosophy* makes a case for Schmitt's Catholicism having a constitutive effect on his political thought. As Michael Hollerich points out, however, Schmitt's own fellow Catholics thought otherwise; see Hollerich, *Carl Schmitt*, 118–20. Schmitt's personal relationship with the Catholic Church was strained by the Church's refusal to annul his first marriage in the 1920s.

53. Tunander, "Swedish-German geopolitics," 451.

54. Tunander, "Swedish-German geopolitics," 453.

ernmental politics. Ethno-politics is not biologically fixed and stagnant, however, but is always dynamic. As a living organism, the state is itself a "force and will" that is not bound by nature or by legality.[55] In Kjellén we meet some of the same decisionism, therefore, that is commonly associated with Schmitt and other authors of the so-called "conservative revolution." Both Tunander and Göran Dahl have remarked on the similarity of Kjellen's project with that of Schmitt.[56]

The type of integrative nationalism found in Kjellén was meditated to the church in Sweden by such figures as Johan Alfred Eklund, who collaborated with Kjellén on the conservative journal *Det nya Sverige* (The New Sweden). For Eklund the key triumph of the Reformation was the integrated wholeness of Swedish life: "the government of the church and the state now coincide," and "the world of the spiritual life has accordingly become *one*."[57] In Eklund's thought, Sweden and its church were one, a collective personality. The nation-church, or folk church, served as the soul of the state, which derived its legitimacy from the nation-church. Eklund was suspicious of the liberal ideas of neutrality, pluralism, and secularity, because they threatened to drive a wedge between "the most intimate union" of church and nation.[58]

Kjell Blückert's book *The Church as Nation* has detailed how the church in Sweden assimilated nationalist discourse in the early twentieth century. With the rise of abstract individual subjects, disembodied relationships, and larger communities of communicating strangers in the 19th century, nationalism took on an integrative function that had previously belonged to the church. In the transition from a theocratic monarchy to a parliamentary democracy in the 19th century, the state lost its divine ontological status, church hegemony was questioned, and the people or nation became the ultimate point of reference. For figures like Eklund, "The nation became an ecclesial means to restore an ideal

---

55. Tunander, "Swedish-German geopolitics," 453–58.

56. Tunander is primarily concerned to show how some of Schmitt's' geopolitical concerns—especially his idea of a European *Grossraum*—are anticipated in Kjellén. Göran Dahl makes the connection between Schmitt and Kjellén in his article "Will 'The Other God' Fail Again? On the Possible Return of the Conservative Revolution," 42–43, 46.

57. Eklund, *Andelivet i Sveriges kyrka*, 37, 69, quoted in Blückert, *Church as Nation*, 175.

58. Blückert, *Church as Nation*, 192–98.

unity in society, a unity that should be incarnated, or at least summed up, by the church."[59] The danger, however, is that the church would no longer legitimize the common values of the society, but would be legitimized by them. The national church adopted the concept "folk church" as a way to "regain solidarity from the incarnate people."[60] The nation and nation-state would come to replace the church as the bearer of unity. As Blückert puts it, nation as church would come to replace church as nation. "The change is caught in the following illuminating observation: Earlier the church had sacraments *in* the society, now the church depicts itself as a sacrament *for* the society."[61]

After World War II, the more overt nationalism became muted, and "society" and "state" more often replaced "nation" as the transcendent point of reference. Nevertheless, the Swedish model of "Folkhemmet" and its attendant folk church continued the quest for wholeness. Some have noticed a resemblance of the Swedish model with Schmitt's attempts to counter the fissiparous effects of liberalism. One author has claimed "The so-called Swedish model was not only the most successful implementation of the ideology of the Conservative Revolution, but also the world's most advanced implementation of a corporativist state."[62] This seems like an odd claim, in that the Swedish model is often associated with the left instead of the right. Nevertheless, an issue of the Swedish journal *Res Publica* has been dedicated to the influence of Schmitt and the other theoreticians of the German "Conservative Revolution" in Scandinavia.[63] There does not seem to be a lot of evidence of direct influence of Schmitt in Sweden. There are, however, certain homologies between Schmitt's thought and the "Folkhemmet": anti-liberalism, decisionist legal theory, emphases on national identity, a strong corporatist state, and the personalization of sovereignty. Although the architects of the post-World War II Swedish model shunned "metaphysics" and sought to base their construction of society on a scientific basis,[64] Schmitt would no doubt be able to recog-

59. Blückert, *Church as Nation*, 21; also 142–43.
60. Blückert, *Church as Nation*, 143.
61. Blückert, *Church as Nation*, 143.
62. von Kreitor, "Conservative Revolution in Sweden."
63. The issue is "Tema Konservativ revolution," *Res Publica* 23 (June 1993).
64. As Arne Rasmusson writes "In the 1920s to the 1960s everyone seemed to accuse everyone else of being 'metaphysical.' There was an agreement that metaphysics was a bad thing, but there was no agreement about what it was"; Rasmusson, "A Century of

nize the "Folkhemmet" as one more secularized theological concept, or, more acutely, a covertly theological concept awaiting full articulation.

My concern is not with Schmitt as such, but with the fate of the typically Christian division of political unity within a state that has such aspirations to wholeness. What happens to the body of Christ when it is incorporated into a state-body such as that envisioned in the Swedish model? The constitution of the church as a "folk church" is meant to resist the kind of privatization to which liberalism aspires. The church remains concerned with the whole of Swedish life. But is the church simultaneously threatened with "rendering harmless the effect of Christ in the social and political sphere"? Does the de-anarchizing of Christianity leave it only "a certain legitimating function" within the state?

The story of the church's adaptation to the welfare state is told in different ways. One way is to describe the welfare state as simply the outworking of the Gospel imperative to form community and care for the weakest members. Bishop Gunnar Stålsett of Oslo has written "The texture of the Nordic welfare state is unambiguously Christian."[65] In a similar vein, the former chairman of the Danish parliament, Erling Olsen, said that "the very idea of the social welfare state is the secularized idea of 'love your neighbor' in Christianity."[66] I am sure that similar sentiments could be found expressed in the Swedish context. Urban Claesson's study of Church of Sweden pastor and Social Democratic member of Parliament Harald Hallén, for example, shows how Hallén interpreted the Kingdom of God in terms of the creation of a righteous socialist society.[67] The story of the church's encounter with the welfare state, however, can also be told in a more melancholy way. As Björn Ryman tells it, optimism about the Christianization of society gave way in the post-World War II period to fears about the secularization of the church.[68] As Ryman and Peter Lodberg point out as well, the welfare state has had a tendency to increase individualism rather than organic solidarity. With each person able to rely directly on the state, older forms of communal solidarity have

---

Swedish Theology," 131.

65. Stålsett, "Foreword," x.
66. Lodberg and Ryman, "Church and Society," 101.
67. Claesson, *Folkhemmets kyrka*.
68. Ryman, "Church of Sweden 1940–2000," 54–56.

been replaced or weakened. The church as a common social network has suffered as a result.[69]

The ecclesiological question that arises in this context is whether the church can rely on the state-body to carry its corporal presence into the world, or whether, instead, the church must be a social—even political—body in its own right, the body of Christ. In other words, the question of the church's encounter with the welfare state is never simply a matter of identifying which social values are truly Christian and judging whether or not they are put into practice by the state. For example, "care for the neighbor," "equality," "personal freedom" and so on are often identified as Christian values, and then the state is judged on these criteria. But the question cannot simply be one of abstract values; it must be a question of concrete social bodies. It is always an ecclesiological question, a question of what kind of social bodies are formed and how authority is mediated through those bodies. The church cannot content itself with being the putative soul of society, while delegating its body to the nation-state. Schmitt rightly implied that the state cannot content itself with the body; it must have the soul as well.

Schmitt was also correct when he said that the key question of church/state relations is "Who decides?" In the United States, we have seen how, in the face of strenuous opposition to the launch of the Iraq War in 2003 by most major church leaders, most Christians were content to let the President decide what counts as a just war. While the Pope, through his envoy to the U.S., called the upcoming war "illegal" and "unjust,"[70] Catholic conservatives were calling for Catholics to leave the decision to George W. Bush.[71] Catholics in the military, with few exceptions, accepted the president's judgment. The distinction between religion and politics allows American Catholics to consider the opinion of the church on the war, but claim that the crucial decision is beyond the church's area of competence. Confidence in the immanent sovereignty of a democratically-elected government effectively negates the sovereignty of Jesus Christ in the realm of the political.

69. Lodberg and Ryman, "Church and Society," 118–19.

70. Cardinal Pio Laghi, quoted in Powers, "Confronting Iraq: Catholic Church View."

71. Weigel, "The Just War Case for the War," 7–10 and Novak, "War to Topple Saddam is a Moral Obligation."

Separation and Wholeness

In Sweden, the homogeneity of the "Folkhemmet" has given way to a more diverse population, and economic liberalism has made inroads. Ecclesiologically, the separation of church and state in 2000 has opened a space to reconfigure the church as a distinct body, and allow the church to be an independent channel of Christ's politics. The question of "Who decides?" remains most acutely, perhaps, in questions about the way that church leaders are elected, and the role that political parties play in those elections.

I have limited specific knowledge about the challenges facing the church in Sweden. I do think, however, that the separation of church and state allows for some creative rethinking about separation and wholeness. On the one hand, the church is called, I think, to live its vocation as the unsettling political presence of Christ's rule in a world that desperately needs the good news that the Kingdom of God has already begun. The church needs to live out the politics of Jesus Christ in ways that will sometimes be in tension with the politics of the world. Gerhard Lohfink says it well:

> The Church could not be the space for redemption and liberation opened by Christ if it were unworldly and saw itself simply as an agency for conveying truth. It must not surrender more and more of its tasks to the state so that, in the end, it is reduced to a watered-down separate department of society responsible only for the rites of passage and marginal situations, or acts as guarantor of the hope for life beyond. The church is about the wholeness of everything there is.[72]

On the other hand, the church's vocation to wholeness means that it cannot become a separate enclave that stands apart from and judges the world from without. The very fact that Christ's rule is cosmic means that the Holy Spirit of Christ blows freely outside the boundaries of the church, and all that is good and true and beautiful there may be held up by the church and made the material for the one all-embracing cosmic Eucharist. At the same time, the church is sinful, and stands under Christ's judgment. But we cannot therefore refuse to avail ourselves of Christ's judgment in the sacraments. To put ourselves under the judgment of the Eucharist is to see political questions in the light of the Kingdom of God, to see, that is, that it is the slaughtered Lamb who rules, and that sovereignty is servanthood.

---

72. Lohfink, *Does God Need the Church?*, 290.

BIBLIOGRAPHY

Augustine. *City of God*. Translated by Henry Bettenson. Harmondsworth: Penguin, 1972.

Blückert, Kjell. *The Church as Nation: A Study in Ecclesiology and Nationhood*. Frankfurt: Peter Lang, 2000.

Brown, Raymond E. *The New Jerome Biblical Commentary*. Englewood Cliffs, NJ: Prentice Hall, 1990.

Brueggemann, Walter. "Old Testament." In *The Blackwell Companion to Political Theology*, edited by Peter Scott and William T. Cavanaugh, 7–20. Oxford: Blackwell, 2004.

Claesson, Urban. *Folkhemmets kyrka: Harald Hallén och folkkyrkans genombrott. En studie av socialdemokrati, kyrka och nationsbygge med särskild hänsyn till perioden 1905–1933*. Uppsala: Uppsala Universitet, 2004.

Dahl, Göran. "Will 'The Other God' Fail Again? On the Possible Return of the Conservative Revolution," *Theory, Culture, & Society* 13, no. 1 (1996) 25–50.

Dulles, Avery. *The Catholicity of the Church*. Oxford: Clarendon Press, 1985.

Eklund, J.A. *Andelivet i Sveriges kyrka: II. Under förtryckets och nydaningens tid*. Stockholm: Sveriges Kristliga Studentrörelses Förlag, 1928.

Gelasius I. "Letter to Emperor Anastasius." In *From Irenaeus to Grotius: A Sourcebook in Christian Political Thought*, edited by Oliver O'Donovan and Joan Lockwood O'Donovan. Grand Rapids: Eerdmans, 1999.

———. "The Bond of Anathema." In *From Irenaeus to Grotius: A Sourcebook in Christian Political Thought*, edited by Oliver O'Donovan and Joan Lockwood O'Donovan. Grand Rapids: Eerdmans, 1999.

Hamburger, Philip. *Separation of Church and State*. Cambridge: Harvard University Press, 2004.

Hobbes, Thomas. *Leviathan: or the Matter, Forme, and Power of a Commonwealth Ecclesiasticall and Civil*. New York: Collier, 1962.

Hollerich, Michael. "Carl Schmitt." In *The Blackwell Companion to Political Theology*, edited by Peter Scott and William T. Cavanaugh, 107–22. Oxford: Blackwell, 2004.

von Kreitor, Nikolai. "Conservative Revolution in Sweden." No pages. Online: http://foster.20megsfree.com/sweden.htm.

Lodberg, Peter, and Björn Ryman. "Church and Society." In *Nordic Folk Churches. A Contemporary Church History*, Björn Ryman et al., 99–121. Grand Rapids: Eerdmans, 2005.

Lohfink, Gerhard. *Does God Need the Church? Toward a Theology of the People of God*. Translated by Linda M. Maloney. Collegeville, MN: Liturgical Press, 1999.

de Lubac, Henri. *The Motherhood of the Church*. Translated by Sister Sergia Englund. San Francisco: Ignatius Press, 1982.

Luther, Martin. "Temporal Authority: To What Extent it Should be Obeyed." Translated by J.J. Schindel. In *Luther's Works*, volume 45, edited by Walther I. Brandt. Philadelphia: Fortress Press, 1962.

———. "To the Christian Nobility of the German Nation." In *Three Treatises*. Luther, Martin. Translated by Charles M. Jacobs. Philadelphia: Fortress Press, 1966.

Meier, Heinrich. *The Lesson of Carl Schmitt: Four Chapters on the Distinction between Political Theology and Political Philosophy*. Translated by Marcus Brainard. Chicago: University of Chicago Press, 1998.

Novak, Michael. "War to Topple Saddam is a Moral Obligation." *The Times* (London), February 12 (2003).
O'Donovan, Oliver. *The Desire of the Nations: Rediscovering the Roots of Political Theology*. Cambridge: Cambridge University Press, 1996.
Potter, David. *A History of France 1460-1560: The Emergence of a Nation State*. New York: St. Martin's Press, 1995.
Powers, Gerald. "Confronting Iraq: Catholic Church View." *Washington Post*, March 7 (2003). No pages. Online:http://www.washingtonpost.com/wp-srv/liveonline/03/special/world/sp_world_powers030703.htm.
Rasmusson, Arne. "A Century of Swedish Theology." *Lutheran Quarterly* XXI (2007).
Ryman, Björn. "Church of Sweden 1940-2000." In *Nordic Folk Churches. A Contemporary Church History*. Björn Ryman et al., 54-56. Grand Rapids: Eerdmans, 2005.
Schmitt, Carl. *Political Theology: Four Chapters on the Concept of Sovereignty*. Translated by George Schwab. Cambridge, MA: MIT Press, 1985.
———. *Roman Catholicism and Political Form*. Translated by Gary Ulmen. Westport, CT: Greenwood Press, 1996.
———. *The Leviathan in the State Theory of Thomas Hobbes: Meaning and Failure of a Political Symbol*. Translated by George Schwab and Erna Hilfstein. Westport, CT: Greenwood Press, 1996.
Skinner, Quentin. *The Foundations of Modern Political Thought*. Cambridge: Cambridge University Press, 1978.
Stålsett, Gunnar. "Foreword." In *Nordic Folk Churches: A Contemporary Church History*, Björn Ryman et al., vii-xi. Grand Rapids: Eerdmans, 2005.
Tunander, Ola. "Swedish-German geopolitics for a new century: Rudolf Kjellén's 'The State as a Living Organism.'" *Review of International Studies* 27 (2001).
Wainwright, Geoffrey. *Eucharist and Eschatology*. New York: Oxford University Press, 1981.
Weigel, George. "The Just War Case for the War." *America* 188, no. 11 (March 2003).
Yoder, John Howard. "To Serve Our God and to Rule the World." In *The Royal Priesthood: Essays Ecclesiological and Ecumenical*. Grand Rapids: Eerdmans, 1994.
———. *The Politics of Jesus: Vicit Agnus Noster*. Grand Rapids: Eerdmans, 1972.

Sacrament as Social Process

Some Historical Footnotes

ARNE RASMUSSON

In 1991 the late Mennonite theologian John Howard Yoder published the article "Sacrament as Social Process: Christ the Transformer of Culture" in *Theology Today*.[1] It originated in some ideas developed in his Stone lectures delivered in Princeton in 1980 and the ideas were further developed in the book *Body Politics* from 1992.[2] In the article, Yoder describes five central Christian practices: baptism, breaking bread, fraternal admonition, the universality of charisma, and the Spirit's freedom in the meeting,[3] and then analyzes the church's life in the world in terms of these practices. One might describe it as a form of sacramental theology. God is present in, through, and under these ecclesial practices. One might say, following Walter Kasper, though Yoder does not do this explicitly, that if Jesus Christ is the primal sacrament, and the church as the body of Christ is Jesus' universal sacrament, then these social practices are the realization of Christ's sacramental presence in the world.[4] Kasper would, of course, define the sacraments differently. A Protestant theologian like Jürgen Moltmann comes even closer to Yoder.[5] One should also note that

---

1. *Theology Today* 48/3 (1991), 33–44. The text is also published in Yoder, *The Royal Priesthood*, 359–73. It is the latter version I am using here.
2. Yoder, *Body Politics*.
3. He partly names these practices differently in *Body Politics*.
4. Kasper, *Theology and Church*, 111–28.
5. Moltmann, *Church in the Power of the Spirit*, 199–206.

Yoder does not take the list of social practices described as exhaustive. It exemplifies central Christian social practices.

However, I will not discuss sacramental theology here. Instead, what I want to do is to take a few historical examples of how both the living of these practices and their misuse have directly or indirectly influenced societies, although they are not and should not be understood as instruments for something else. Thus, this paper simply consists of a few historical footnotes to Yoder's text. The examples I have taken are more or less random, but also examples of which I have some knowledge. Many others could be given, and many other stories could be told. I will also, for reasons of space, spend most time on baptism.

BAPTISM AND THE ONE BODY OF CHRIST

Yoder describes baptism as the entry into a new people that transcends all other given or chosen identities, such as gender, ethnicity, nationality, class, and so on. Baptism is not symbolizing something (as in a Zwinglian view). It is what it represents. He can describe this as a sort of sacramental realism, but he is critical of a sacramental view that separates the sacrament from this social reality and sees baptism as only a transfer of inner grace. It is grace and new birth, but this can never be separated from its social reality, becoming part of the church, Christ's body, which relativizes all other identities. It does not eliminate all differences, but transcends and relativizes them.

This, Yoder says, is the Christian basis for equality. It should be more powerful than the Enlightenment idea that postulates universal equality as self-evident. It is not. Modern racism, based on "scientific naturalism", actually arose among some Enlightenment thinkers. The liberal legal and political theorist Jeremy Waldron notes in his book about John Locke and the idea of human equality that it is very difficult to find actual arguments for equality in contemporary legal and political philosophy, it is just taken as an axiom.[6] He claims that historically the idea of human equality "has been shaped and fashioned on the basis of religion",[7] and more specifically Christian theology. Waldron ends the book in the following way:

---

6. Waldron, *God, Locke, and Equality*, 1–4.
7. Waldron, *God, Locke, and Equality*, 242.

> Equality cannot do its work unless it is accepted among those whom it consecrates as equals. Locke believed this general acceptance was impossible apart from the principle's foundation in religious teaching. We believe otherwise. Locke, I suspect, would have thought we were taking a risk. And I am afraid it is not entirely clear, given our experience of a world and century in which politics and public reason have cut loose from these foundations, that his caution and suspicions were unjustified.[8]

Today it is difficult to find philosophers, scientists, or politicians who question human equality outright, but during the nineteenth and the first half of the twentieth century it was common among liberals, conservatives, and socialists, as well as among "scientifically enlightened" Christians. A common argument was that science (especially Darwinism) had emancipated us from dated and dangerous dogmas about human equality. This led to the dominance of racist views that were crucial for the legitimation of racism, colonialism, and the eugenic movement that in part supported the euthanasia movement. Such views lost much of their acceptance after 1945, because of the use fascism and Nazism made of them.[9] This history supports Waldron's and Yoder's claim that human equality is not something we just can take for granted. But, of course, neither has equality been taken for granted within Christendom. Locke made his argument with other Christians, although at that time the issue was not racial, but social inequality. And more important than Locke's theological and philosophical arguments for equality, or what made these arguments possible, was the practices of certain dissenting Christians.

When the church became more or less identical first with the Roman Empire, and later with Medieval European Christendom, and later again, with modern nations and nation-states, and baptism became compulsory, baptism changed meaning. It was understood as the transferring of internal grace, but this had little to do with daily living. The sacramental economy had become a separate sphere.[10] However, not entirely. Baptism was also understood as a mark of being part of Christendom, or later Europe, or Sweden.

---

8. Waldron, *God, Locke, and Equality*, 243.

9. Fredrickson, *Racism*, Mosse, *Toward the Final Solution*, Hawkins, *Social Darwinism in European and American Thought, 1860–1945*, Weikart, *From Darwin to Hitler*, and Dowbiggin, *A Concise History of Euthanasia*.

10. Cf. Kasper, *Theology and Church*, 122–25.

What happened in South Africa is a well known example of the historical outworking of this idea.[11] The Dutch settlers who came to the Cape in the seventeenth century had for a long time lived with the idea of baptism as, in effect, a sign of being European. Anyone with a European parent was, for the colonial government, eligible for baptism. One took Old Testament rules about slavery seriously, so it meant that one had to set baptized slaves free (though they had to pay for the education and other things they had received) after a certain number of years. Because slave owners usually were not especially interested in freeing their slaves, they seldom let them be baptized. Baptism thus functioned as an ethnic sign that separated Europeans from Africans, and became a reason for opposition to missionary work among Africans.

However, other Christians, first Moravians, did not accept this and started mission work among Africans against strong opposition from the Dutch Reformed.[12] At the same time, the practice of baptism was also crucial for the struggle of churches against racism and separation. To take just one example: the 1924 Synod of the Anglican Church in South Africa criticized its own internal practice in terms of "the Brotherhood of all in Christ, the equality of all before God, and the unity of the body."[13] It did not live up to its confession, but the baptismal unity was used as a basis for criticism.

The practice of making baptism a civil or ethnic sign of inclusion/exclusion is also part of Yoder's critique of compulsory infant baptism.[14] During the Middle Ages, baptism was still understood as incorporation into Christendom, the universal Church. After the Reformation, baptism became increasingly incorporation into a national body. In her book on nationalism, Liah Greenfeld makes the beheading of Sir Thomas More, because of his refusal to accept the king's absolute supremacy, the symbolic watershed between Christendom and modern nationalism.

> Sir Thomas More was a Christian; this was his identity, and all his roles, functions, and commitments that did not derive from it (but were implied, for example, in being a subject of the king of

---

11. For the following, see e.g. Elphick and Davenport, *Christianity in South Africa* and De Gruchy and De Gruchy, *The Church Struggle in South Africa*.

12. For more details, see especially Gerstner, "A Christian Monopoly."

13. Cited in De Gruchy and De Gruchy, *The Church Struggle in South Africa*, 36.

14. Cf. Moltmann, *Church in the Power of the Spirit*, 226–42.

> England) were incidental to it. The view that 'one realm' could be a source of truth and claim absolute sovereignty was, to him, absurd. 'Realms' were but artificial, secondary divisions in the ultimately indivisible body of Christendom.[15]

He was unable "to deny what seemed to him plainly evident."[16] For his judges it was different. Protestantism thus became the midwife of modern nationalism. At the other end of this development, nationalism

> acquired its own momentum; it existed in its own right; it was the only way in which people now could see reality and thus became reality itself. For nationalism was the basis of people's identity, and it was no more possible at this point to stop thinking in national terms than to cease being oneself.[17]

The body of the nation was experienced as much more real than the body of Christ, the universal church. The churches thus had to understand and justify themselves in terms of the national body.

When in the nineteenth and early twentieth century the self-evident German and Nordic Lutheran churches were challenged by secularizing and modernizing changes and movements and secular nationalism (and in a country like Sweden by the Free Church movements), they answered by developing explicit folk church conceptions that drew on nationalist ideologies and practices. For the theological creators and supporters of this theology, infant baptism was the essential ecclesial practice.[18] Baptism thus continued as a nationalist practice.

This nationalism, which the churches helped create and strongly supported and legitimated, would have fateful consequences in the twentieth century. It in part created the war culture that made the First World War more or less inevitable, which was followed by the Second World War and the Holocaust, the Cold War, and so on.[19] But few theologians

---

15. Greenfeld, *Nationalism*, 30.
16. Greenfeld, *Nationalism*, 30.
17. Greenfeld, *Nationalism*, 87.
18. Cf. Billing, *Den svenska folkkyrkan*, 14. Billing had some second thoughts when he saw what happened in Germany, see pp. 142. A more clearly nationalist folk church theology is found in Eklund, *Andelivet i Sveriges kyrka, 10 Vol*. See further Blückert, *The Church as Nation*.
19. Keegan, *A History of Warfare*, 21, Elias, *The Germans*, Nipperday, *Religion Im Umbruch*, and Rasmusson, "Historicizing the Historicist."

or church leaders have seen this as a scandal, as a betrayal of baptism, of the body of Christ, because for most it has simply been self-evident that the primary body is the nation. The German Roman Catholic theologian Gerhard Lohfink has written:

> The Church did not prevent the two world wars, and could not prevent them. They simply broke over it. But what is disturbing today is something beyond the mere fact of the two wars: the Church is the body of Christ, beyond all boundaries, the people of God among the nations. That in 1914 Christians went enthusiastically to war against Christians, baptized against baptized, was not seen in any way as destruction of what the Church is in and of its very nature, a destruction that cried out to heaven. That was the real catastrophe.[20]

Of course, there were in 1914 some who thought otherwise. Karl Barth was one. The theological revolution he started began with his horror over the churches' and the theologians' celebration of the war and their own nations, but also with his deep disappointment with the failure of the international labor movement to resist nationalism.[21] A church in Europe or in South Africa that at least to some extent had lived the reality of Christian baptism could have been a radical political testimony. It might have changed the world much more than anything else that the church could have done or said.

But few churches have questioned the primacy of the national body. Even the transnational Roman Catholic Church often succumbed to nationalism. So often did also so called Free churches. In America, for example, one could say that radical Protestant individualism combined with denominationalism in practice made America itself the church of a semi-Christian civil religion.[22]

Adrian Hastings, in his history of nationalism, writes that it "is groups like the Mennonites and the Quakers which have produced a Christian spirit most impervious to nationalism" and which have produced "the most creative efforts . . . to free Protestantism and Christianity with it from

---

20. Lohfink, *Does God Need the Church?*, 315.
21. Rasmusson, "Church and Nation-State."
22. Cf. Hatch, *Democratization of American Christianity*. For a recent affirmative discussion of America's role in God's providence, see Webb, *American Providence*.

nationalist bondage."[23] In the case of Mennonites, the Anabaptists, this started with a renewed practice of baptism that separated baptism from national membership. For the later Quakers, one could say that they practiced the reality of baptism, although they were not a baptismal church. Or one could say that it was their practice of two of the other practices Yoder mentions, also central for Anabaptists: the Spirit's freedom in the church meeting and the universality of gifts of the Spirit, which led to similar consequences.

We saw that Yoder claimed that the reality of baptism was more important for equality than Enlightenment philosophy. The issue of slavery is an example.[24] Slavery has been a universal institution. It existed everywhere. It was a normal and legitimate part of society. The interesting issue is not how anyone could have defended it, but why at some time and place some started to question and fight it. The modern struggle against slavery was not primarily driven by Enlightenment philosophers. Some of them supported slavery. Thomas Jefferson, who wrote the American declaration of independence, stating that everyone is created equal, had slaves.

It was mainly Christians who worked against slave trade and slavery, but not just any Christians. Slavery had disappeared from most parts of Europe, but in the colonies in the Americas and in Africa it was reinstituted. As in South Africa, some American Christians were uneasy about it at first. The same issue as in South Africa was raised here. What happens if they are baptized? Is enslaving baptized Christians allowed? Soon, however, theologians found their way around this issue.

The first public protest against slavery in the English colonies came in 1688 from newly arrived Mennonites.[25] Later on it was the more numerous and more centrally placed Quakers and evangelical Christians who took the lead, both in America and in England. In England, Quakers, evangelical Anglicans, and Methodists were a main force behind the first modern social movement, the struggle against the slave trade and slavery. Similar groups struggled against slavery in America.[26]

23. Hastings, *Construction of Nationhood*, 205.
24. For the following, see e.g. Stark, *For the Glory of God*, 291–365.
25. "Minute against Slavery."
26. In addition to Stark, see e.g. Dayton, *Discovering an Evangelical Heritage*, Hochschild, *Bury the Chains*, and Brown, *Moral Capital*. Of course, many other Christians had condemned slavery, including many popes, but it was Quakers, Methodists, Evangelicals, and their like, who were crucial for the creation of the social movements that struggled

Again, it is church practices—baptism combined with the freedom of the Spirit in the church, and the universality of charisma—that lie behind this.

BREAKING BREAD TOGETHER

For Yoder, breaking bread together, a real, not a ritualized, meal, embodies "basic economic sharing among the members of the messianic community," and a critique of social stratification, which in turn "is the promise of newness on the way for the world."[27]

The history of South Africa again provides a tragic example of the refusal to break bread together. One might say that apartheid was created when the body of Christ was split apart at the Lord's Table, with white people refusing to share the meal with Africans.[28] In the nineteenth century also the Dutch Reformed were active in mission work among Africans. Baptizing Africans into the church was no longer questioned. In 1838 the British Parliament finally abolished slavery in the colonies. When white Christians refused to share the meal with Africans, the 1829 Synod of the Dutch Reformed Church declared that the meal "was to be administrated 'simultaneously to all members without distinction of colour or origin' because this was 'an unshakable principle based on the infallible Word of God.'"[29]

However, in 1859 the Synod did accept separation at the table. It was still described as an anomaly, a weakness, a temporary concession to "weak" European Christians, but it led to the division of the church along racial lines. Soon enough this division was understood as normal and even as prescribed by the created order. One might say that one of the crucial sources of apartheid ideology was the theological attempt to defend the separate Eucharist tables.

Sharing a meal, and not just a ritualized and individualized meal, makes it more difficult to keep others out of the rest of one's social and economic life. If one separates at the table, one also separates in the rest of life and it will be much easier to live in a lie about the life of the others.

---

against the slave trade and slavery during the eighteenth and nineteenth centuries.

27. Yoder, *Body Politics*, 21.

28. See again Elphick and Davenport, *Christianity in South Africa* and De Gruchy and De Gruchy, *Church Struggle in South Africa*.

29. De Gruchy and De Gruchy, *Church Struggle in South Africa*, 7.

Paul says in 1 Cor 11 that when economic inequality is taken into the breaking of the bread, the body of Christ is denied and God will judge the church.

THE SPIRIT'S FREEDOM IN THE MEETING

For Yoder, another central practice is the church meeting. According to Yoder, every Christian has received the Spirit and the gifts of the Spirit. Anyone is allowed to talk in the church and take part in decision making. The Spirit leads the church through the common conversation. As it is said in Acts 15: "it seemed good to the Holy Spirit and us." Yoder has written a well-known essay called "The Hermeneutics of peoplehood,"[30] in which he discusses Christian hermeneutics as a social process. To understand the hermeneutical process it is, he argues, more important to understand social processes than how "thought" functions. This is crucial for the politics of the church. "The multiplicity of gifts is a model for the empowerment of the humble and the end of hierarchy in social process. Dialogue under the Holy Spirit is the ground floor of the notion of democracy."[31]

It is often noted that this practice in some churches contributed to Western democracy. It was one factor. Its importance relative to other factors is, of course, debated. People learned what might be called the democratic habits in the church meetings: giving and listening to arguments, being ready to accept being outvoted, the idea of one person, one vote, and that everyone has a vote, and not least the right to dissent. In his classic discussion of democracy, A. D. Lindsay wrote "that the inspiration of modern democracy came from men's experience of the ... character of democratic government in the Christian congregation—came therefore especially from the Independents, the Anabaptists, and the Quakers."[32] Moving these practices to the level of national governments involved many changes, a theme central to Lindsay's discussion. But he also thought that democratic politics presupposes "a society of democratic non-political associations."[33]

---

30. Yoder, *Priestly Kingdom*, 15–45. Cf. Fowl and Jones, *Reading in Communion*.
31. Yoder, *Royal Priesthood*, 364.
32. Lindsay, *Essentials of Democracy*, 20.
33. Lindsay, *Essentials of Democracy*, 0 (sic). For a similar argument for the case of Sweden, see Lundkvist, *Folkrörelserna i det svenska samhället 1850–1920*. See further for

Against this one might mention how the church took up and internalized for example the structures of the Roman Empire, of Byzantium, of the modern centralized and absolute state, or of modern economic corporations and how this in turn has influenced the political, social, and cultural structures of Christendom and the modern world.

There are of course many problems with "democracy" as such, as political scientists or proponents of less democratic churches remind us. Democracy without a common context, a common good and a telos—in Christian terms, without the word of God, the holy Spirit, and a church that together want to follow Jesus Christ—easily falls into individualism, majoritarianism, and power struggle, which leads to manipulation and the death of political discourse, as seen, for example, at election times. In Alasdair MacIntyre's terms, an external good (power) corrupts the internal good of politics (the communal—even conflictual—work for the common good).[34] Lindsay claims that this, as he describes it, debased practice of democracy has been given theoretical support in another tradition, one that tried to fashion politics and social theory after physics and therefore began with a form of atomistic individualism. This tradition runs, says the socialist Lindsay, from Hobbes to English utilitarians and French Encyclopaedists as well as to Marxist socialism, and still, one could add, shapes much social science.[35]

A story unknown to most people is the struggle against slavery in West Africa. It is told in Lamin Sanneh's book *Abolitionist Abroad: American Blacks and the Making of Modern Western Africa*.[36] Slavery was very common in African societies. The Western slave trade could exist

---

different perspectives on this ambiguous process, Stackhouse, *Creeds, Society, and Human Rights*, Hatch, *Democratization of American Christianity*, Fogel, *Fourth Great Awakening and the Future of Egalitarianism*, and Himmelfarb, *Roads to Modernity*. Yoder discusses Christianity and democracy in *Priestly Kingdom*, 151–71. Cf. also Milbank, *Future of Love*, 242–63 and the comment by philosopher Jürgen Habermas, often described as the greatest defender of the "unfinished Enlightenment project": "I would not object if someone were to say that my conception of language and my communicative concept of action oriented to reaching understanding are nourished by the legacy of Christianity. The 'telos of reaching understanding' . . . may well draw on the legacy of the Christian understanding of the logos, which is, after all, embodied in the communicative practice of religious congregations (and not just the Quakers)." Habermas, *Time of Transitions*, 161.

34. MacIntyre, *After Virtue*, 174–83.
35. Lindsay, *Essentials of Democracy*, 1–6.
36. Sanneh, *Abolitionists Abroad*.

because slavery and slave-trading were already well established before first the Muslim slave traders and then, several centuries later, Western traders began to trade with African suppliers.

Sanneh claims that it was the missionary efforts of African American ex-slaves and Africans, shaped by Christian convictions and practices woven together with the ideas of the American Revolution (with its mixture of various Enlightenment and Christian roots), that were behind African abolitionism. It was a result of the church's mission. Sanneh describes an ecclesial evangelical faith and practice that promoted an antistructure undermining the monarchical political establishment of the West African chiefdoms. In this process the antislavery movement became an indigenous movement. "With the antislavery campaign," Sanneh writes, "something new and permanent was attempted in African societies, and that represented a significant enough break with the old political morality."[37]

Sanneh stresses in this book that it was not traditional Christendom churches that were behind this, but non-established, non-Christendom churches, similar to the types that were behind the struggle against the slave trade and slavery in England and America, such as Quakers and Evangelicals. The older European mission, shaped by Christendom, had allied itself with the traditional African chieftain structures. The newer evangelical mission, led by African American ex-slaves and Africans, created a bottom-up anti-structure that elevated "freed slaves, ex-captives, women, and other despised members of society into positions of leadership and responsibility."[38] That is, the practice of the church meeting.[39]

THE UNIVERSALITY OF CHARISMA

Behind Yoder's understanding of the church meeting is what he calls the "the universality of Charisma." Every member of the church is gifted, empowered, by the Spirit (1 Cor 12 and 14, Rom 12, and Eph 4) for the common good. The Spirit is "present in, with, and under a particular pattern of social process," which Yoder thinks leads to a practice "different both from contemporary available social models and from most of

---

37. Sanneh, *Abolitionists Abroad*, 10.
38. Sanneh, *Abolitionists Abroad*, 18.
39. Cf. also for some broader implications, Sanneh, *Whose Religion Is Christianity?*

what later Christian history has done with the notions of 'charisma' and 'ministry.'"[40]

This implies for Yoder a critique of a separate priesthood, but also of a radical individualism where everyone is exchangeable and where there is no real common good. He can say that we have only seen pale images of it in practice. But one can also say that this is behind the understanding of the church meeting we mentioned. It can function as a space for disempowered people, a place where they have a voice. A place where everyone has a task. When this giftedness is held down, new orders or new churches have been created.

It has also empowered women. There are signs of the latter in the early church, and then again and again through history in different Christian movements. Women empowered by the Spirit. When these movements were institiutionalised, patriarchy took over again. In modern times, we see part of the origin of feminism in some Christian churches, in the USA often the same that struggled against slavery. The biblical arguments for the subordinate role of women were often the same as the arguments for slavery. In the more established churches, the structures for ordination were often rigid, but among for example Baptists, Methodists, Quakers, and Holiness churches women were given leading roles in the early nineteenth and even the late seventeenth century. It was recognized that they were empowered by God's spirit. The same happened on a smaller scale in Sweden. [41] In America, Oberlin College, which had its origin in the second Awakening and Charles Finney, was the first college with common education for women and men. Later, some of these churches have done an about turn and are now among the most patriarchal.[42]

FRATERNAL ADMONITION

Yoder also talks about Fraternal Admonition—about discipline, repentance and forgiveness. He refers to the secular Jewish philosopher Hannah Arendt, otherwise often quite critical of Christianity, who said: "Without being forgiven, released from the consequences of what we have

---

40. Yoder, *Royal Priesthood*, 363. This theme is developed further in his book *Fullness of Christ*.

41. One example is described in Gunner, *Nelly Hall*.

42. MacHaffie, *Her Story*, and Dayton, *Discovering an Evangelical Heritage*, esp. 85–98.

done, our capacity to act would, as it were, be confined to one single deed from which we could never recover; we would remain the victims of its consequences forever."[43] She also says that "The discoverer of the role of forgiveness was Jesus of Nazareth."[44]

South Africa and the Truth and Reconciliation Commission led by Bishop Desmond Tutu are, of course, again an obvious example of an attempt to use this practice, not perfectly, not in a totally Christian way, but in a way that has become an example for others. The combination of truth and reconciliation is crucial in a Christian understanding of forgiveness. Would such a process be conceivable in a totally non-Christian context?[45]

Another example is the work done by the sociologist John Paul Lederach, professor of International Peace Building and involved in conciliation work in countries like Colombia, the Philippines, Nepal, Tajikistan, and several African countries. He has helped design and conduct training programs in 25 countries. He is a Mennonite and influenced by the theology of Yoder, but in the context of Mennonite practices of reconciliation. His starting point is the practices of reconciliation he learned in church.[46]

CONCLUSION

The practices described are all central for Christianity and intrinsically connected to basic Christian convictions.[47] It is common practices that constitute the church as a social body. As Yoder notes, there is nothing strange or esoteric about them. They are ordinary human practices. But the church believes that they are also acts of God. God is acting in, with, and under these practices. These practices are furthermore public, accessible for anyone. They are, fundamentally, not separate "ritual" or "religious" practices. Neither were they, Yoder says, "revealed from above or created from scratch; each was derived from already existent cultural

---

43. Arendt, *Human Condition*, 213.

44. Arendt, *Human Condition*, 214f. For Yoder's reference to Arendt, see Yoder, *For the Nations*, 30f.

45. Tutu, *No Future without Forgiveness*, De Gruchy, *Reconciliation*.

46. See e.g. Lederach, *Moral Imagination*, Lederach, *Journey toward Reconciliation*, and Sampson and Lederach, *From the Ground Up*.

47. Yoder, *Royal Priesthood*, 369–73.

models . . . yet in the gospel setting they have taken on new meanings and a new empowerment."[48] They are constitutive of the life of the church as the body of Christ in the world.

For Yoder, this understanding of the church provides a fruitful perspective for understanding the life of the church in the world. The most important thing the church can do "for the sake of the world" is simply to be the church, to live these practices in its own life. That in itself shapes the societies in which the church lives, though one may not know how beforehand, just as the church's denial of them does. In certain situations, these practices may lead to various forms of social activism. At other times, other communities may take up parts of these practices. The examples I have mentioned are historically quite visible, but at the time few thought about these historical consequences, positive or negative. Similarly, most important is the ordinary, not very visible or dramatic, life of local congregations baptizing, sharing the meal, debating in the church meeting, encouraging the gifts of its members, and dealing with conflicts and forgiving each other. It does not require a common language or general acceptance of specific theological construals, and it is not a question of attempting to control the world. It requires presence. These practices are not, Yoder concludes, "ways to administer the world; they are modes of vulnerable but also provocative, creative presence in its midst. That is the primordial way in which they transform culture."[49]

---

48. Yoder, *Royal Priesthood*, 371.

49. Yoder, *Royal Priesthood*, 373. For a further discussion of Yoder's social theology, see Rasmusson, "Revolutionary Subordination."

FOR THE SAKE OF THE WORLD

BIBLIOGRAPHY

Arendt, Hannah. *The Human Condition.* New York: Doubleday, 1959.
Billing, Einar. *Den svenska folkkyrkan.* Stockholm: Sveriges kristliga studentrörelses förlag, 1930.
Blückert, Kjell. *The Church as Nation: A Study in Ecclesiology and Nationhood.* Frankfurt am Main: Peter Lang, 2000.
Brown, Christopher Leslie. *Moral Capital: Foundations of British Abolitionism.* Chapel Hill: University of North Carolina Press, 2006.
Dayton, Donald W. *Discovering an Evangelical Heritage.* New York: Harper & Row, 1976.
De Gruchy, John W. *Reconciliation: Restoring Justice.* Minneapolis: Fortress Press, 2002.
De Gruchy, John W., and Steve de Gruchy. *The Church Struggle in South Africa.* Minneapolis: Fortress Press, 2005.
Dowbiggin, Ian. *A Concise History of Euthanasia: Life, Death, God, and Medicine.* Lanham: Rowman & Littlefield, 2005.
Eklund, J. A. *Andelivet i Sveriges kyrka, 10 vol.* Stockholm: Sveriges kristliga studentrörelses bokförlag, 1911-1938.
Elias, Norbert. *The Germans: Power Struggles and the Development of Habitus in the Nineteenth and Twentieth Centuries.* New York: Columbia University Press, 1996.
Elphick, Richard, and T. R. H. Davenport (eds.). *Christianity in South Africa: A Political, Social, and Cultural History.* Berkeley: University of California Press, 1997.
Fogel, Robert William. *The Fourth Great Awakening and the Future of Egalitarianism.* Chicago: University of Chicago Press, 2000.
Fowl, Stephen E., and L. Gregory Jones. *Reading in Communion: Scripture and Ethics in Christian Life.* London: SPCK, 1991.
Fredrickson, George M. *Racism: A Short History.* Princeton: Princeton University Press, 2002.
Gerstner, Jonathan N. "A Christian Monopoly: The Reformed Church and Colonial Society under Dutch Rule." In *Christianity in South Africa: A Political, Social, and Cultural History,* edited by Richard Elphick and T. R. H. Davenport, 16-30. Berkeley: University of California Press, 1997.
Greenfeld, Liah. *Nationalism: Five Roads to Modernity.* Cambridge: Harvard University Press, 1992.
Gunner, Gunilla. *Nelly Hall: Uppburen och ifrågasatt: Predikant och missionär i Europa och USA 1882-1901.* Uppsala: Svenska institutet för missionsforskning, 2003.
Habermas, Jürgen. *Time of Transitions.* Cambridge: Polity Press, 2006.
Hastings, Adrian. *The Construction of Nationhood: Ethnicity, Religion, and Nationalism.* Cambridge: Cambridge University Press, 1997.
Hatch, Nathan O. *The Democratization of American Christianity.* New Haven: Yale University Press, 1989.
Hawkins, Mike. *Social Darwinism in European and American Thought, 1860-1945: Nature as Model and Nature as Threat.* Cambridge: Cambridge University Press, 1997.
Himmelfarb, Gertrude. *The Roads to Modernity: The British, French, and American Enlightenments.* New York: Vintage books, 2005.
Hochschild, Adam. *Bury the Chains: Prophets and Rebels in the Fight to Free an Empire's Slaves.* Boston: Houghton Mifflin, 2005.
Kasper, Walter. *Theology and Church.* London: SCM, 1989.
Keegan, John. *A History of Warfare.* New York: Alfred A. Knopf, 1993.

Lederach, John Paul. *The Journey toward Reconciliation.* Scottdale: Herald Press, 1999.
———. *The Moral Imagination: The Art and Soul of Building Peace.* Oxford; Oxford University Press, 2005.
Lindsay, A. D. *The Essentials of Democracy.* 2nd ed. London: Oxford University Press, 1935.
Lohfink, Gerhard. *Does God Need the Church? Toward a Theology of the People of God.* Collegeville: Liturgical Press, 1999.
Lundkvist, Sven. *Folkrörelserna i det svenska samhället 1850–1920.* Stockholm: Almqvist & Wiksell International, 1977.
MacHaffie, Barbara J. *Her Story: Women in Christian Tradition.* 2nd ed. Minneapolis: Fortress Press, 2006.
MacIntyre, Alasdair C. *After Virtue: A Study in Moral Theory.* Notre Dame: University of Notre Dame Press, 1981.
Milbank, John. *The Future of Love: Essays in Political Theology.* Eugene: Cascade Books, 2009.
"A Minute against Slavery, Addressed to Germantown Monthly Meeting, 1688." Quaker Heritage Press. Online: www.qhpress.org/texts/oldqwhp/as-1688.htm. (Last updated 2007. Accessed 2009-05-02.)
Moltmann, Jürgen. *The Church in the Power of the Spirit: A Contribution to Messianic Ecclesiology.* New York: Harper & Row, 1977.
Mosse, George L. *Toward the Final Solution: A History of European Racism.* London: J.M. Dent, 1978.
Nipperday, Thomas. *Religion im Umbruch: Deutschland 1870–1918.* München: Verlag C. H. Beck, 1988.
Rasmusson, Arne. "Church and Nation-State: Karl Barth and German Public Theology in the Early 20th Century." *Ned Geref Teologiese Tydskrif* 46: 3–4 (2005) 511–24.
———. "Historicizing the Historicist: Ernst Troeltsch and Recent Mennonite Theology." In *The Wisdom of the Cross: Essays in Honor of John Howard Yoder*, edited by Stanley Hauerwas et al., 213–48. Grand Rapids: Eerdmans, 1999.
———. "Revolutionary Subordination: A Biblical Concept of Resistance in the Theology of John Howard Yoder." In *Peace in Europe, Peace in the World: Conflict Resolution and the Use of Violence*, 35–67. Wien: Iustita et Pax Dokumentation, 2002.
Sampson, Cynthia, and John Paul Lederach. *From the Ground Up: Mennonite Contributions to International Peacebuilding.* New York: Oxford University Press, 2000.
Sanneh, Lamin O. *Abolitionists Abroad: American Blacks and the Making of Modern West Africa.* Cambridge: Harvard University Press, 1999.
———. *Whose Religion Is Christianity? The Gospel Beyond the West.* Grand Rapids: Eerdmans, 2003.
Stackhouse, Max L. *Creeds, Society, and Human Rights: A Study in Three Cultures.* Grand Rapids: Eerdmans, 1984.
Stark, Rodney. *For the Glory of God: How Monotheism Led to Reformations, Science, Witch-Hunts, and the End of Slavery.* Princeton: Princeton University Press, 2003.
Tutu, Desmond. *No Future without Forgiveness.* New York: Doubleday, 1999.
Waldron, Jeremy. *God, Locke, and Equality: Christian Foundations of John Locke's Political Thought.* Cambridge: Cambridge University Press, 2002.
Webb, Stephen H. *American Providence: A Nation with a Mission.* New York: Continuum, 2004.

Weikart, Richard. *From Darwin to Hitler: Evolutionary Ethics, Eugenics, and Racism in Germany.* New York: Palgrave Macmillan, 2004.

Yoder, John Howard. *Body Politics: Five Practices of the Christian Community before the Watching World.* Nashville: Discipleship Resources, 1992.

———. *For the Nations: Essays Evangelical and Public.* Grand Rapids: Eerdmans, 1997.

———. *The Fullness of Christ: Paul's Revolutionary Vision of Universal Ministry.* Elgin: Brethren Press, 1987.

———. *The Priestly Kingdom: Social Ethics as Gospel.* Notre Dame: University of Notre Dame Press, 1984.

———. *The Royal Priesthood: Essays Ecclesiological and Ecumenical.* Grand Rapids: Eerdmans, 1994.

Space, Materiality and the Politics of Leaving
Church of Sweden and Rosengård's Social Segregation

HENRIK WIDMARK

Take the main road south from Malmö city, Amiralsgatan, and you will eventually pass under Rosengård's suburban center. When this center, named Ro-cent, was built in the mid 1960s, an article in the magazine *The Art of Building* compared Amiralsgatan to the river Arno in Florence, and Ro-cent to Ponte Vecchio, with its symbolic values of trade, prosperity and unity.[1] Ro-cent was seen as the space that held the city together and just as crossing the river Arno in Florence was an act of unity, so the centre was to consolidate Malmö and Rosengård. In Renaissance Florence, the Ponte Vecchio was the principal crossing, expressing the thriving city state's unity and turning the river from a disruption and a border into an opening; something similar was envisaged about Ro-cent and Rosengård. At that time, in 1960s, Rosengård was seen as a space of modernity where the modern Swedish welfare state manifested its victory over poverty, unhealthiness, segregation and, above all, raised hopes for the future—it was a modern Florence shaped in welfare.[2] The district church of Rosengård, in Church of Sweden's Västra Skrävlinge parish, was a vital element in this building of space and constitution of a new place. That was also the case in most of the new suburbs that were constructed in the decade 1965–74, when Sweden made a gigantic effort to overcome a housing shortage and succeeded in building one million homes.[3] Many of the brand-new hous-

1. Sjöö, "Nya Rosengård," 28–35.
2. Rosengård as a space of hope and modernity see Ristilammi, *Rosengård*.
3. For the million housing programme see e. g. Hall, *Rekordåren*.

ing areas were sited on undeveloped land, with little evidence of a former history that could give the place significance. Ideally, the spirit of community in these new neighborhood units would be built on the sense of belonging and knowing your neighbors. But it also relied on commerce, municipal services and the church caring for the souls of the inhabitants. In these ventures, Church of Sweden, together with the municipality and commercial forces, was a major material and social actor in constructing space and constituting place. In Rosengård, that meant that the real-estate construction company erected a church complex in Ro-cent and rented it to the church.[4] The municipal facilities and the commercial areas were provided in the same way. Thus, the modern welfare neighborhood districts were built on a commercial basis, with all the social amenities of a modern state. Consequently the church was a part of everyday life in Rosengård right from the start. However, Rosengård's center, Ro-cent, was not intended just for the area's residents; it was also meant to serve the southern parts of Malmö and thus be a major hub that linked up the modern city's various districts. In the prosperous, forward-looking years of the late 1960s, Church of Sweden was one of the builders and organizers of the new suburban public spaces that were meant to strengthen the unity of society.

Being a constitutor and an organizer of the suburb of Rosengård, the church has an obligation to its parishioners and to society as a whole to care for and mediate a space that does not end at the suburb's geographical borders. Through the imagination of the body of Jesus Christ, the church at its best should live up to the popular device of "acting local, thinking global" and consequently be a part of the local society and connect local place to global space.[5] When we look at what became of the "suburbs of prosperity" this is especially important, because the church is also partly responsible for the suburb's legacy and the lives that form its place in history and build its space of the future.

AFTERMATH OF A SOCIETY IN CHANGE

Barely a decade later, these spaces of modernity and prosperity, with their pioneering spirit, experienced the rapid and brutal decline and fall of Malmö's industrial era and the effects of a post-Fordist economic recon-

4. Länsstyrelsen, *Bostadsmiljöer*, 124.
5. See Cavanaugh, *Being Consumed*, 87–88, for how this could be practiced.

struction, and they were soon to experience the effects of post-Keynesian reorganizations of the welfare state.[6] The imagery rapidly turned into segregation, anonymity and dissolution.[7] Malmö's situation started to improve in the postmodern economy at the turn of the millennium, but in Rosengård things went from bad to worse and there was absolutely nothing left of the 1960s bright prospects. It was not just the inhabitants who were disillusioned; civil society itself seemed to feel alienated and when immigrants became the majority group a not always well-disguised xenophobia changed Rosengård from a problem area into, to allude a term of Michel Foucault, a negative heterotopia—a space of harmful difference.[8] At this point, Church of Sweden chose to leave its material setting in Rosengård and de-consecrate the church.[9]

In spring 2007 Rosengård was burning. Media reported on a war in the suburbs of Malmö.[10] Once again, reports of violence, poverty, exclusion and people feeling betrayed by society filled the news—and once again Rosengård was the focal point. Rioting is always a sign of failure, a sign of a society failing to imagine itself as one. The American congresswoman Maxine Waters made the problem of rioting understandable when she talked about the Los Angeles riots of 1992: "I am angry. It is alright to be angry. It is unfortunate what people do when they are angry. The fact of the matter is, whether we like it or not, riot is the voice of the unheard."[11] And Rosengård's inhabitants probably have one of the weakest voices in Sweden today. There will be more fires in Rosengård, and more riots.[12] Rosengård will become even more marginalized; the feeling of not belonging—not to Malmö, not to Sweden or any other community that respects and gives hope and empowers its citizens—will just grow stronger and stronger day by day. In this "Neighborhood of Exile," Church

6. See Stigendal, *Varför*, 20–38, Val, *Cities in Decline*, 71–78, and Billing, *Skilda världar*. Compare Massey, *World City*, 17–19, Sernhede, *Alienation*, 28–49, and Waquant, *Urban Outcasts*, 170–71.

7. Sandström, *Rosengård*. For an early account of how the imaginary changed see Flemström and Ronnby, *Fallet Rosengård*.

8. On Hetherotopia Foucault, "Of other Spaces," 13–30.

9. Rehnquist, "Kyrkan flyttar."

10. Nilsson, "Vilda Upplopp," Whaldén, "Nya bränder," and Ekelund, "Nya våldsamheter."

11. Deveare Smith, *Twilight: Los Angeles*, 162.

12. Further riots in Rosengård broke out at Christmas 2008.

of Sweden chose to resign and to leave its only material and symbolical space of belonging—its place of worship. To leave is a decision—with consequences; it is a statement willingly or unwillingly—it is a political act.

THE ACT OF LEAVING

On Wednesday the 15th of March 2000 the congregation in Rosengård church celebrated a service of closing down. A church service could be seen as the embodiment of what the church is, and thus it should inspire to engage in the local parish, as well as in the global community of mankind. The service is a possibility to consider the space of Rosengård as part of something larger than the local geography of social and economic exclusion. This time, however, it did not stimulate engagement in Rosengård. The symbolic meaning of the service was something completely different—a service of the dismissal of the congregation of Rosengård. The gathering of the congregation to celebrate in Rosengård church on that Wednesday evening became an act of redefining the space of Church of Sweden, the parish of Västra Skrävlinge and the space of Rosengård.

As I see it, and in the words of geographer Doreen Massey, it is important that "we recognize space as always under construction."[13] Understanding space in this way opens up to the possibilities of engagement and acting and it also implies that theology and liturgy will have effects on space and thus on the people who are a part of the space. This Exodus dispatched Church of Sweden to the part of Swedish society from which Rosengård had been alienated. The act could be seen as a strategy, in the sense of acting as a part of civil society, where regrouping and financial considerations became more important—as part of the parish's overall strategy—than being materially present in Rosengård center as a worshiping community.[14] Leaving the material premises of Ro-cent, taking down the church bells that had signaled the church's presence, became an act of segregation. The space of Rosengård lost a central trajectory that had connected it to Christianity and to Swedish society; at the same time, it underlined the experience of the area's social immobility. An article by the chairman of the church council made it evident that

13. Massey, *For Space*, 9.
14. On strategy see de Certeau, *Practice*, 35–36.

Church of Sweden was a part of Swedish society, different from the immigrant society of Rosengård.[15] The writer was outraged by accusations that Västra Skrävlinge turned its back on Rosengård; some contributors to the debate had even said that the parish acted like an apartheid regime. These accusations were, of course, unfair and incorrect but the words he and the accusers used made it clear how the map should be read. He talked about two immigrant churches, by which he meant the Roman Catholic Church and, interestingly enough, Rosengård's Muslim congregation. This implied that Church of Sweden was not an essential part of the immigrant society of Rosengård. The mediated image of Rosengård was a place constituted by immigrants who did not understand and did not culturally comprehend Swedish society. He also wrote about what the church ordinance obliged the parish to do. It was in many ways an official statement that arranged the spaces of the church as a territorial parish with certain obligations that could be carried out within the limits of the church ordinance, and it was a lament of a church that did not feel it belonged in the heterotopia of Rosengård. The article was written with the best intentions and probably not meant to be analyzed, but it nevertheless reflected an identity of the church that constituted, not just its own space as part of Swedish society, but the space of Rosengård as segregated from the same society.

But let us remember that the parish did choose to leave. It made a decision and closed down the church. The act of leaving was dealt with as a problem of redundancy. There were too few parishioners; maintaining a place of worship was too expensive when the parish had another church not all that far away.[16] The church in Rosengård was a negative item on the church's expense account. This argument, which became public in the local paper and on local television, is based on the assumption that redundancy—having too many facilities in which to celebrate mass—is primarily a financial issue. Buildings are just buildings and can be treated as a financial matter. Giving notice of ending the lease of Rosengård church was a legal and financial procedure that the rental arrangements in Rosengård center had made possible. If the church had been owned by Church of Sweden, the problem of redundancy would have looked different, which is not to say that the outcome would have been differ-

15. Björklund, "Kränkande beskyllningar."
16. Björklund, "Kränkande beskyllningar," Rehnqvist, "Kyrkan flyttar."

ent. In reality, however, the effects on Rosengård and on the identity of Church of Sweden, or the effects of the absence of a church in Ro-cent, is first and foremost not a financial but a political and theological issue of how and why the church should be present in the spaces of marginality in Sweden. It is also a question of how space and place are constructed and understood and why the act of leaving changed the imagery of space in Rosengård.

SPACE

Space, and to some extent place, are the key concepts for understanding the politics of leaving as presented here. To explain how I use the term space, I draw on the theoretic that Doreen Massey presented in *For Space*. She formulates three propositions for understanding space:

> First we recognize space as the product of interrelations, as constituted through interactions, from the immensity of the global to the intimately tiny. Second, that we understand space as the sphere of the possibility of the existence of multiplicity in the sense of contemporaneous plurality, as the sphere in which distinct trajectories coexist, as the sphere therefore of coexisting heterogeneity. Third, that we recognize space as always under construction.[17]

Understanding Church of Sweden and Rosengård as spaces or parts of spaces opens up possibilities to act and makes it evident that theology and the identity of the church matter for how these spaces work and are conceived.

I also want to raise another aspect of space, one that theorists of space are not always that keen to mention, namely the meaning of the material milieu, how building and public place are rooted in the locality of place and make a difference to how space is imagined. One of the foremost experiences of being human is that everything takes place. Everything we do is set in a material environment, be it nature, a building or a sidewalk, for instance. These places and buildings are understood, to use the trialectics of the philosopher Henri Lefbvre, through our *spatial practices*—for instance in working, walking or worshiping but also through the buildings and their forms that frame our potential to act. Through the *representations of space*, how these spaces have been imag-

---

17. Massey, *Space*, 9.

ined and mediated. And through *representational space*, how these places and spaces through our imagination have been given meaning, or, as Lefebvre puts it: "space as directly lived, through its associated images and symbols and hence the space of inhabitants and users . . . It overlays physical space, making symbolic use of its objects."[18] It is also important to note that the economy and the politics of a society form geographies.[19] In the case of Rosengård, it is a geography that has become segregated socially and economically weak. This is a geography with factual borders, where on a map you can point out the frontiers to parts that are socially and economically stronger. If you want to imagine this geography as part of a larger space with possibilities for change, you have to be inside and act within the locality of place. To understand how place and space matter in the case of the Rosengård church, one has to consider two central features: the meaning of the church building, and how we conceive the territorial parish of Västra Skrävlinge.

THE BUILDING

A building is an abstraction of its materials, as Rosengård church was of concrete and bricks.[20] It holds no meaning by itself. It makes a difference only when it is comprehended in the context of history, society, religion and spatial practices. Seen as space, it is filled with symbolical and practical meanings. It frames the possibilities of everyday practices as well as imagination, it makes a difference. Rosengård church was a part of the constituent history of Rosengård. It was only the small bell-tower and brick ornamentation that singled out the cube-shaped building from the suburban centre as a place with a specific connotation. What made it a church and evidence of the presence of Church of Sweden in Rosengård was the worshiping congregation. Whether five or fifty persons celebrated mass on Sunday was not the point. Its essential meaning was its presence in the neighborhood centre and its symbolic belonging to all the residents of Rosengård, ideally to all the residents of Malmö.

---

18. Lefebvre, *Production of Space*, 38f.

19. Harvey, *Spaces of Global Capitalism*, Massey, *Spatial Divisions*, and Smith, *Uneven Development*.

20. Hardly nothing is written about Rosengård church, except a few sentences in, Malmö Kyrkliga Samfällighet, *Kyrkor*, 15.

A church building does not have to be situated in the centre, but in the case of Rosengård, where the vast majority of the inhabitants do not belong to Church of Sweden, being in the centre opened up the possibility of being a potentially free space, where the church could act as something relevant to the whole community. Being there and being seen as a worshiping community in Rosengård, where alienation from Swedish society is always at hand, made the church both a trajectory into Swedish society and a tactic of an alternative understanding of the church and Rosengård.[21] This tactic of celebrating mass in Rosengård centre could have enabled the church to be something more than just another part of Sweden' civil society, that so often was believed not to care for the residents of Rosengård. By being in the centre, Church of Sweden made a political statement of belonging—and as a church it is essential to show a presence as a worshiping community and through its symbolical representation in the church building. Leaving the centre underlined the boundaries in Swedish society; it emphasized Rosengård's social segregation; it made the uneven geography of society more evident. The parish did continue to have localities within the imagined space of Rosengård but they were not places of worship, and thus it was harder for the church to communicate the difference of being a church and the difference of belonging to the body of Jesus Christ.

Let us look at another example of the importance of the symbolical space of the suburban centre. On the 6th of January 1986, the Roman Catholic Church celebrated mass in Rosengård centre during the inauguration of the new parish of *St:a Maria i Rosengård (Saint Mary in the Rose Garden)*.[22] Although the Roman Catholic Church already had a small chapel and a parish centre in the district, the symbolical and factual center of Rosengård gave imaginary support to the idea of being a new parish for the whole of Rosengård. The inauguration benefitted from the embedded meaning of the centre. It presented the church as a part of Rosengård in everyday life, as well as a part of the festivities and celebrations of its residents. Eventually the parish built a new church on the outskirts of Rosengård, but at that point the Roman Catholic Church was seen as a natural part of the area—and did not need the symbolical space of the centre to reveal its presence. And not having the history of

21. On tactics see de Certeau, *Practice*, 38.
22. http://www.maria-rosengard.com/KKR/historik_sv.html> retrieved 20080821.

Space, Materiality and the Politics of Leaving

being a national church helped to homogenize inside the marginality of Rosengård.

Ro-cent is embedded with meaning and the place is formed by its layers of history. The place is a collection of its histories so far.[23] Rosengård church is a part of its history—its departure makes it a part of Rosengård's history of loss—a history that forms part of the memory that upholds the area's segregation and dissolution. When Church of Sweden celebrated mass in Rosengård church, it was a part of the space of Rosengård, the simultaneity of the suburb, and at the same time it widened the simultaneity into the existence of eternity. The presence of the Eucharist confirmed the everyday life of the parish as well as unity at a local and a universal level.[24] Thus, Rosengård through its symbolical spaces and the celebration of mass formed a space of hope, at the same time defining the local and breaking down the imaginary borders that isolate the socially and culturally segregated district. A space was constructed ". . . as the product of interrelations, as constituted through interactions, from the immensity of the global to the intimately tiny," to cite Massey.[25] Consequently, leaving a built space conveyed meaning to the local society and to the idea of Church of Sweden's place in Rosengård and in the multicultural community of Malmö.

THE TERRITORIAL CHURCH

The organization of Church of Sweden into territorial parishes, with at least one church building as each parish's symbolical and often factual centre is based on the idea of imagined communities and geographical borders.[26] It is imagined as a community in the sense in which Benedict Anderson writes about nations: "It is Imagined" by the parishioners because "in the minds of each lives the image of their communion."[27] This is how the historical Church of Sweden was formed as a part of the building of a nation and a civil society. In its prime, this system also meant that the imagination of the parish was empowered by the fact that a major part of its population celebrated together once a week. The church building

23. Massey, *Space*, 130.
24. Cavanaugh, *Being Consumed*, 5.
25. Massey, *Space*, 9.
26. Compare Anderson, *Imagined*.
27. Anderson, *Imagined*, 6.

was a living representation of Christ our Savior and at the same time a sign of what held the nation and the local society together. Today, society is organized and understood differently, but Church of Sweden today is still built on the premise that it is an open folk church where everybody, members and non-members, is free to participate and imagine the communion of the parish. Consequently, the space of the parish should be constructed by both members and non-members of the church. If the territorial parish is to remain valid, a common understanding of the presence of the church must be upheld within its spatial borders.

Rosengård belongs to the parish of Västra Skrävlinge and its name presents the first challenge to territorial unity. Västra Skrävlinge refers to the historical municipality of the same name and to the old church village.[28] Commonly the name today is to be understood as the 19th-century church with its allusions to medieval forerunners. It is not in anyway synonymous with Rosengård. But its principal territorial setting is Rosengård. The name is an active part in the construction of borders within the space of the parish, separating most of the parish territory from where the worshiping congregation meets. This separation is underlined by Inre Ringvägen, a major road that physically and mentally separates the parish church from Rosengård, thereby cutting the church off from the greater part of its territorial extension. If Västra Skrävlinge is to uphold the validity of the territorial parish, it is essential that the imagined parish and its material borders are in accordance with each other. That is not the case today and Västra Skrävlinge church accordingly stands as a symbolical explanation of why Church of Sweden has no imagined territorial parish in Rosengård. Space and place do not fit together and the validity of the territorial church is definitely weakened.

Today, the parish of Västra Skrävlinge, of which Rosengård forms the major part in terms of territory and the number of persons living there, is the parish in Church of Sweden that has the smallest number of residents as its members.[29] Off course this does not say anything about the numbers of souls celebrating mass, but it does reflect the problem and the liability of being a folk church in Rosengård. If the church wants to have a presence inside Rosengård, it has to find ways either of not being

28. Wahlbom, *Västra Skrävlinge*.
29. Unsigned, "Toppen och botten."

restricted by how to uphold a territory or of connecting the symbolical space of Västra Skravlinge to the space of Rosengård.

Leaving the church building in the suburb centre amounted to giving up the territory of Rosengård, so the church has to act by connecting to the space, not by referring to the territorial church. Of course, ways can also be found of making Västra Skrävlinge church and the church village a part of the imagination of Rosengård. Today, the old church village only exists as the church and the churchyard; it constitutes a relic from the rural era before the city grew, when Sweden and the church were seen as one and when Rosengård did not exist. This could be both an asset and a problem. It could connect Rosengård to the history of the place, but at the same time it can be a symbol of something incomprehensible with today's Rosengård. Reworking the imagination of Västra Skrävlinge seems to be a much harder task than finding ways of dealing with the church's territorial basis, even though there are no formal ways of abolishing it.

The church seldom speaks of its materiality in buildings or of the physical extension of parishes as means of political and theological practice. When buildings are mentioned, it is usually in terms of economics or heritage. Economics is reflected in the dichotomy between church buildings as history and museums on the one hand, and on the other the care of the people of the church. Moreover, church buildings are mentioned as the nation's or the local place's heritage, as something that primarily matters to the local folk lore society and art historians. Even the idea of the territorial parish system has been frequently discussed as a question of economics or heritage. The case of Rosengård and the closing down of Rosengård church makes it apparent that place matters and that buildings and the territorial church are part of how the space of civil society is organized, as well as a question of theology and politics. At the same time it is apparent that Rosengård and similar neighborhoods of exile do not necessarily benefit from upholding the territorial parish. A possible way to be a part of Rosengård and at the same time counteract the geographies of exclusion is to imagine space as open, but by doing so also leave the territorial borders of the parish behind while upholding the presence in the locality of place. The imagination of space and the presence of buildings to celebrate mass affect the identity of the church and the possibilities of theology, thus they are political.

MULTICULTURALISM

Finally, speaking about Rosengård, churches and segregation brings up the question of multiculturalism.[30] In a community such as Rosengård, where local-national identities of immigrants clash with the national identity of Sweden, where a sense of belonging does not easily fit into either of these identity claims, an open-minded attitude to multiculturalism is indispensible.[31] In practice this makes it necessary to imagine space, in the words of Doreen Massey, "as the sphere of the possibility of the existence of multiplicity in the sense of contemporaneous plurality; as the sphere in which distinct trajectories coexist."[32] This was also one of the Church's major political challenges in Rosengård.

Rosengård church, like many churches in Sweden's socially marginalized suburbs, was multicultural in many senses. Working inside Rosengård required an understanding of other cultures and respect for their right to express themselves. The church as a worldwide body has all the benefits and possibilities of being multicultural, but by leaving the spaces where this, at its best, is part of everyday life denies the church the possibility of expressing this global core. The global begins in the locality of place, and to be able to confront the advantages and disadvantages of the global era means that you have to take an active part in local society.[33] Practicing multiculturalism, where difference is an asset, not a problem, demands more than one part.[34] It means acting and existing on an equal basis. Minority is not the issue in a multicultural integration of Rosengård. Or could it be that what is needed is an integration of Malmö and the Swedish society in Rosengård? Religion must of course be seen as a basis of a multicultural society. To fully comprehend this, material spaces can enlighten the existence of a prism of religion as the backbone of a multicultural society. Today, the Islamic community in Rosengård is

---

30. On multiculturalism and my use of the term see Parekh, *Rethinking Multiculturalism*, Hall, "Conclusion: the Multi-cultural," 209–41, and May, "Multiculturalism," 124–44.

31. Appadurai points out that "globalization is not the process of cultural homogenization." Appadurai, *Modernity*, 9. In the case of Rosengård this means that strong local-national identities prevail among the inhabitants and when old and new identities meet it creates new ones instead of a homogenized global identity.

32. Massey, *Space*, 9.

33. On the changing aspects of the local in a global era see Appadurai, *Moderninty*, 178–99.

34. How hard this is, is well described in Žižek, *Violence*, 47–49.

represented by Malmö Mosque and a few so called basement-mosques housed in club premises. The Roman Catholic Church is represented by St. Mary's Church. Both the major mosque and the Roman Catholic Church are situated on the outskirts of Rosengård, physically close to Västra Skrävlinge church—but spatially separated by the imagination. Both the Islamic centre and the Roman Catholic Church are possible parts of the identity of a migrant and multicultural society. The territorial parish of Church of Sweden has, as mentioned earlier, Rosengård within its borders on a map. But imaginary borders and the identity of belonging to marginality construct the space of Rosengård, thus leaving Church of Sweden outside. Rosengård church in the centre had a historical tie to the construction of Rosengård and thus formed the place. It was placed in the only common physical space shared by all of Rosengård. From that point, celebrating the Eucharist, and acting as part of everyday life, Church of Sweden was a part of both the history and the practiced life of Rosengård, and thus it acted as a part of the multicultural society of the neighborhood. Celebrating mass in Rosengård binds powerful ties to a global and universal experience with possibilities to some extent weaken the segregation and marginalization. It is not primarily a missionary act, but an act as a church to belong to society and all its parts. The built milieu matters; when practiced, it is a possible way to build a truly multicultural society. But placed on the other side of imaginary borders, it does not matter or at its worst it becomes a counterproductive representation.

A SENSE OF BELONGING

The descriptions of Rosengård presented earlier in this paper and in research are generally dark and without hope. Poverty and redundancy through the reorganization of the economy has affected a majority of the immigrants and eventually become a stigma that has trapped the suburb's residents as outcasts on the marginality of Swedish society.[35] The state and local government has initiated programs to stop segregation and deprivation and fight crime and poverty in the large post-war housing estates. Local organizations, including churches, have also been active in fighting the problems in these stigmatized areas. In Rosengård, large efforts have been made to improve social conditions and the material milieu. But still

---

35. Sernhede, *Alienation*, 28–54, Lindén and Lindberg, *Immigrant Housing*, 98–115. Compare Wacquant, *Urban Outcasts*, 169.

the problems seem to grow day by day. In the early days of the housing estates in Rosengård, the social problems were blamed on the built milieu.[36] This critique has continued, but as more immigrants moved into the area this was considered to be a further alienating stigma.[37] The possibilities of multiculturalism have been noted but seldom acted on.

But Rosengård has urban qualities seldom found in Sweden. The use of a common shared public space within the housing estates in Rosengård generates a social life with social control capable of encouraging meetings within the smaller community. But these are enclaves within the larger district, and their internal solidarity results in a pattern of numerous sub-units, organized by the taxonomies of everyday life. The space of these sub-units has few trajectories that lead into the civil Swedish community, and is often held together by ethnic ties that form the spaces on a global scale. But it is a global space with weak connections to local place. The sub-units form as diasporas organized on a global scale through a mass-mediated imagery where the local outside the sub-units, and definitely outside Rosengård, becomes even more alienated.[38] In this situation it seems that both the local and the universal have been detached from the life of the residents. What is left is fragmentation within the suburb and segregation from the outside, the only thing that holds the residents together is estrangement from Swedish society.

In this lived experience, Church of Sweden chose to leave, to make its presence invisible. This was a political act that cannot be undone. But what can be done is to seek possible ways to visualize the worshiping congregation, within the imaginary of Rosengård, and again be a part of the ever-changing spaces of exile, where it seems, it should be a Christian duty to be.

POST SCRIPTUM

At Christmas 2008, after this text had been written, Rosengård was burning again. This time the riots started when a cellar mosque was evicted. Eight years after Church of Sweden left its building, it seems that the premises of religion matter in Rosengård. This calls for a final reflection on Rosengård church and raises the question of why there were no riots

---

36. On the early critique see Franzén and Sandstedt, *Grannskap*, 17–25.
37. See e.g. Fjelman Jaderup "Amiralsgatan," Jönsson, "Efter Bränderna."
38. On diasporas and imagination see Appadurai, *Modernity at Large*, 6.

Space, Materiality and the Politics of Leaving

when the church closed. Did the church not matter, or did it not belong in Rosengård? The reasons why people do or do not riot are not always easy to comprehend, and worship and buildings are seldom the only reason for heightened tension in troubled neighborhoods. Moreover, there are major differences between a small cellar mosque and a church building that represents the national church. However, an essential difference between the two places of worship and their religious communities is that one was evicted, while the other chose to leave. To be able to choose to leave means that you have a choice of belonging. The decision to leave implies participating from the outside in the organization of the geography of Rosengård as a place of estrangement; a segregated space. To be forced to leave is just another tragic effect of the marginalization and alienation that at its worst leads to violence. In the end, what brings the church and the mosque together is that they are both part of what has made the space of Rosengård in to an even darker negative Heterotopia.

BIBLIOGRAPHY

Anderson, Benedict. *Imagined Communities.Reflections on the Orgin and Spread of Nationalism*. London: Verso, 1991

Billing, Peter. *Skilda Världar? Malmös 1990-tal i ett kort historiskt perspektiv*. Malmö: Malmö stad, 2000.

Björklund, Elly. "Kränkande beskyllningar om Rosengårdskyrkan." *Sydsvenska Dagbladet*, 19 April (2000).

Cavanaugh, William T. *Being Consumed. Economics and Christian Desire*. Grand Rapids: Eerdmans 2008.

de Certeau, Michel. The *Practice of Everyday Life*. Berkley and Los Angeles: University of California Press, 1988 (1984).

Deveare Smith, Anna. *Twilight: Los Angeles 1992*. New York: Anchor/Doubleday, 1994.

Ekelund, Martin. "Nya våldsamheter." *Aftonbladet*, 17 April (2007).

Foucault, Michel. "Of other Spaces." In *Heterotopia and the City: Public Space In a Postcivil Society*, edited by M. Dehaene and L. de Cauter, 13–30. London: Routledge, 2008.

Fjelman Jaderup, Elin. "Amiralsgatan i ny skepnad ska ge liv åt Rosengård. Stadsplanering nytt grepp mot sociala problem." *Sydsvenska Dagbladet*, 28 August (2008).

Flemström, Carin and Alf Ronnby. *Fallet Rosengård. En studie i svensk planerings- och bostadspolitik*. Stockholm: Prisma, 1972.

Franzén, Mats and Eva Sandstedt. *Grannskap och Stadsplanering. Om stat och byggande i efterkrigstidens Sverige*. Uppsala: Acta Universitatis, 1981.

Hall, Stuart, "Conclusion: the Multi-cultural question." In *Un/Settled Multiculturalisms*, edited by B. Hesse, 209–41. London: Zed Books, 2000

Hall, Thomas. *Rekordåren. En epok i svenskt bostadsbyggande*. Karlskrona: Boverket, 1999.

Harvey, David. *Spaces of Global Capitalism. Towards a Theory of Uneven Geographical Development*. London: Verso, 2006.
Jönsson, Dan. "Efter bränderna i Rosengård." *Dagens Nyheter*, 23 December (2008).
Lefebvre, Henri. *The Production of Space*. Oxford: Blackwell Publishing, 1991 (1974).
Lindén, Ana-Lisa and Göran Lindberg. "Immigrant Housing Patterns in Sweden." In *Urban Housing Segregation of Minorities in Western Europe and United States*, edited by Elisabeth D Huttman et al., 92–115. Durham: Duke University Press, 1991.
Länsstyrelsen. *Bostadsmiljöer i Malmö. Inventering*. Del 3: 1965–1975. Malmö: Länsstyrelsen.
Malmö Kyrkliga Samfällighet, *Kyrkor i Malmö*. Malmö, 1989.
Massey, Doreen. *For Space*. London: Sage Publications, 2005.
———. *Spatial Divisions of Labour. Social Structures and the Geography of Production*. London: Macmillan, 1985.
———. *World City*. Cambridge, UK: Polity Press, 2007.
May, Stephen. "Multiculturalism." In *A Companion to Racial and Ethnic Studies*, edited by David Theo Goldberg and John Solomos. London: Blackwell Publishing, 2002.
Nilsson, Kerstin. "Vilda upplopp hela helgen i Malmöstadsdelen." *Aftonbladet*, 16 April (2007).
Parekh, Bhikhu. *Rethinking Multiculturalism. Cultural Diversity and Political Theory*. Basingstoke: Macmillan, 2000.
Rehnquist, Pia. "Kyrkan flyttar." *Sydsvenska Dagbladet*, 31 May (2000).
Ristilammi, Per-Markku. *Rosengård och den svarta poesin. En studie av modern annorlundahet*. Stockholm: Symposium, 1999.
Sandström, Lasse. *Rosengård i medieskugga. Om medier som medel och hinder för integration*. Stockholm: Stiftelsen för mediestudier, 2005.
Sernhede, Ove. *AlieNation is my Nation. Hiphop och unga mäns utanförskap i det nya Sverige*. Stockholm: Ordfront, 2002.
Sjöö, Manthe. "Nya Rosengård blir Malmös största bostadsområde." *Tidning för Byggnadskonst* (1965).
Smith, Neil. *Uneven Development. Nature Capital and the Production of Space*. Athens: The University of Georgia Press, 2008 (1984).
Stigendal, Mikael. *Varför finns Malmö? Krisen i ett historiskt perspektiv*. Malmö: Malmö stad, 1996.
Unsigned. "Toppen och botten i Svenska kyrkan." *Dagens Nyheter*, 13 August (2008).
Val, Natasha. *Cities in Decline? A Comparative History of Malmö and Newcastle After 1945*. Malmö: Malmö Högskola, 2007.
Wacquant, Loïc. *Urban Outcasts. A Comparative Sociology of Advanced Marginality*. Cambridge UK: Polity Press, 2008.
Wahlbom, Hans. *Västra Skrävlinge. En sockens historia*. Malmö: Västra Skrävlinge församling, 2000.
Wahldén, Christina. "Nya bränder I Rosengård." *Svenska Dagbladet*, 18 April (2007).
Žižek, Slavoy. *Violence. Six sideways reflections*. London: Profile Books, 2008.

Social Agent—a Queer Role for the Church

NINNA EDGARDH

Jesus preached to the crowds saying:

> Love your enemies, do good to those who hate you, bless those who curse you, pray for those who abuse you. If anyone strikes you on the cheek, offer the other also; and from anyone who takes away your coat do not withhold even your shirt. Give to everyone who begs from you; and if anyone takes away your goods, do not ask for them again. Do to others as you would have them do to you.[1]

Jesus' message is a queer one in a Western world dedicated to personal success and self-fulfillment. But it is not just a message from an idealist prophet in a bygone time. It is a way of life, a social practice, that is still carried out by in many places around the world, often by people associated with Christian churches. It is a practice at odds with the times, a lively faith practice in an age when the institutional churches are often regarded as relics of an ancient past, at least in Western Europe. But it is also a problematic practice in many respects. It is highly gendered in that it is primarily carried out by women. It is often belittled, even by the churches themselves and referred to inferior sectors separated from the more highly valued sectors of liturgy and dogmatics.

Now the differences between the European and North American situation regarding church and welfare is striking in many ways. As summarized in *Religious America, Secular Europe* by Peter Berger et al.

> In Europe, it is axiomatic (almost) that the state should take responsibility for the basic needs of the population. It is this assump-

---

1. Luke 6:27–31.

tion, moreover, that underpins the 'welfare state'—an essentially positive term strongly associated with the notion of solidarity. The welfare state becomes thereby a significant aspect of European heritage, both paralleling and, in many respects, continuing the traditional role of the majority church.[2]

The authors continue to explain that all of these assumptions are different in the U.S., where no state church is to be found, and not even a state in the European sense, and where the very word welfare has somewhat other connotations than in Europe. While welfare in most European countries is understood as something positive, to strive towards, it might in the U.S. easily be understood as a waste of the tax payers money and while welfare provision in Europe is positively connected to collectivism and egalitarianism, in the U.S. it is rather connected to individualism and free enterprise.[3]

This being said, it is important to underline that the phenomenon discussed in the article, welfare provided by faith based organization, exists in both contexts, but might well be interpreted differently. The argumentation in the article is based on the European situation, for the simple reason that the research it is built on has been performed in Europe.[4] The main argument is that the gendered and neglected way of life, exemplified in the welfare provision offered by Christian churches and organizations, contains an hitherto not fully recognized potential for European church traditions, increasingly challenged by the effects of secularization. It is however not only a resource for the churches, but even more so for late-modern European societies, where consumerism and the law of the market today threaten some of the basic humanitarian values on which the ideals of the European welfare states have been built.

The examples of Christian social practices that constitute the starting point of the article have been documented in a comparative European research project called *Welfare and Religion in a European Perspective*. The project, here called the Welfare and Religion Project, aimed at studying the role of the European majority churches in the different welfare systems operating in Europe today. All the major church traditions of

2. Berger et al., *Religious America, Secular Europe*, 87.

3. Berger et al., *Religious America, Secular Europe*, 87f.

4. The article has been produced with the support of The Linnaeus Research Program *The Impact of Religion—Challenges for Society, Law and Democracy*.

Europe were covered; i.e. Catholic, Orthodox, Anglican and Lutheran (more specifically German Lutheran-Reformed and Nordic Lutheran). The results are based on qualitative case studies carried out in medium-sized towns in eight countries: Sweden, Norway and Finland in the North; England, France and Germany; and Italy and Greece in the South.

Details about the theories, methods and results of the project may be found in two final reports that will appear at Ashgate 2009/2010.[5] The aim here is to take a step back from these details, and present a reflection upon the results from a more overarching ecclesiological point of view. The theoretical tools for the analysis will be fetched, as the title suggests, from queer theory, and even queer theology. This may be seen as a thought experiment, to explore what such a perspective may contribute in addition to more traditional ways of approaching ecclesiological issues.

QUEER PERSPECTIVES

Queer has become a generic term for theoretical approaches in research that question taken-for-granted positions regarding gender and sexuality. In its original sense, queer means differing from what is usual or normal. More specifically, it is used to characterize that which is seen as perverted or sexually deviant and in this sense it has become a derogative term for homosexuals, an insult. In a development similar to how "gay" and "black" previously have been turned from insults to positive labels, queer as insult has lately been turned on its head and adopted as a positive identification marker. As such it has been especially connected to demands for increased tolerance for varieties of sexual identities and behaviors. However, unlike gay and black, queer is not intended to mark a stable identity, defined by sexuality or race. Queer is fluid. It is more of a verb than a noun. It thus belongs to the type of gender theory that has developed in recent decades, where gender is understood in terms of ongoing constructions rather than as stable identities or properties. Queer turns our attention towards the deviation from the norm rather than towards identity. Thereby it invites us to observe linguistic and social practices that are normally obscured, because they are taken for granted. In that way, queer perspectives facilitate our questioning of this normality.[6]

---

5. Bäckström et al., *Welfare and Religion: Volume 1*, and Bäckström et. al. *Welfare and Religion: Volume 2*.

6. Turner, *Genealogy of Queer Theory*.

Against this background, the authors of a recent anthology on *Queer Theology* find queer theory useful as an invitation to theological reflection. The editor of *Queer Theology*, Gerard Loughlin, makes use of queer perspectives to invoke aspects of the Christian tradition that do not fit into the normality of the modern world. Theology is, according to Loughlin, "a queer thing . . . for theology runs counter to a world given over to material consumption, that understands itself as 'accidental', without any meaning other than that which it gives to itself, and so without any fundamental meaning at all."[7]

This queer dimension of theology is, however, according to Loughlin, not new. Even when theology was culturally dominant it was queer, for theology has always sought the strange as it has "sought to know the unknowable in Christ".[8]

What this article wants to explore is the extent to which a queer theological perspective may be of help in the ecclesiological reflection needed today, when church traditions meet new challenges in the social field. The basic idea is that churches as social agents in the late-modern Western culture take on a queer role, in the sense of a role that is strange and deviating from the cultural norm. What would be queerer today than women and men unselfishly serving others instead of looking for personal success and self-fulfillment? But queer should not be used too lightly to characterize difference in general. At first sight, church-related voluntary social work seems, of course, to have very little or anything to do with sexuality. Still, the role as social agent is a queer role for the church, not only because it is odd in relation to a society dedicated to other values, but because the role actually has dimensions that are connected to gender and sexuality. These are problematic dimensions for the churches today, as revealed in the range of contested issues connected to these areas, from abortions to same-sex unions. The argument of the article is that the churches might be helped in their dealings with these issues, by seeing and accepting their role as queer, rather than by identifying as protectors of a traditional value basis, with the heterosexual nuclear family as its primary symbol.

---

7. Loughlin, "Introduction: The End of Sex," 7.
8. Loughlin, "Introduction: The End of Sex," 7.

Social Agent—a Queer Role for the Church

INSULT TURNED ON ITS HEAD

The connection between the church's role as social agent and gender and sexuality may be illustrated by a Swedish example. In Sweden we have for some time heard warnings against the development of a feminized caregiver church, casually adapting to current demands. The church has been likened to a cleaning lady, who does the dirty work that nobody else wants to take on, and who takes care of those who are no longer wanted in a society increasingly geared to efficiency. The implications behind the imagery include social work being traditional women's work and thus of little or low value. This gendering in turn presupposes a dichotomy between what men do and what women do, a dichotomy that according to modern gender theory has a lot to do with heteronormative ideals, presupposing attraction between women and men as one, or even *the* major driving force in social life. What queer theology might inspire us to do is to turn the alleged insults of the imagery on their head, by letting the role of the caregiver and guardian of the little ones be freed from its misogynist and derogative connotations. Washed in the biblical texts about Jesus and queered in the shared Eucharistic meal, the church as defender of outcasts may in this way be resurrected as an ideal for Christian discipleship, male and female. As such it will be at odds with much of the modern world, but not separated from it. It will be marginalized in a society dedicated to the ideal of the autonomous individual, but still it will be anchored in the very centre of the mission of Christ in the world.

FOR THE SAKE OF THE WORLD

The argument will be developed more at length below with the help of material from the research project and from queer theology. A good starting point is presented in the very title of the book; *For the Sake of the World*. What is this sake of the world? What does it look like from the perspective of welfare provision? What is at stake concerning welfare in Europe?

Welfare has to do with the provision of basic security in life: economic and social safety, adequate housing, medical care, education and so forth.[9] Europeans have traditions and high expectations of these things

---

9. For an elaboration of possible contemporary understandings of the concept "welfare" see Pettersson, "Majority Churches as European Welfare Agents."

being provided communally. In a country like Sweden, this occurs primarily through tax-financed services provided by the state. In Germany, it is organized through a thorough social security system in close collaboration between the state and civil society, including the churches. In southern Europe, represented in the Welfare and Religion Project by Italy and Greece, the organization is still much more informal and the extended family carries a lot of the responsibility, supported by churches and other civil society organizations. The state is here more of a back-up, although sometimes not a very effective one.

Common to all these ways of organizing welfare is the conviction that basic security for all should somehow be provided in a communal way. This conviction is closely related to the historic role of the Christian churches in Europe, which have in different ways contributed to the development of social care, health care and education. In this way the churches have been highly influential in the development of the European welfare states in their different varieties. During the last century, however, the role of the churches has been privatized and spiritualized, at least until quite recently, because what we see in the results from the project is demands for a new public role for the churches, related to a range of ongoing social changes, confronting the post-war European welfare systems. Some of these changes are positive effects of the present welfare systems, like the increase in the average life span, which creates new strains in both the care for elderly people, in the health care system and in the labor market, where a diminishing labor force is supposed to provide for increasing numbers of elderly and young people.

Other challenges have to do with the transition to a late modern society, based on a service economy increasingly dependent on global financial interests. While this economy tends to bring hitherto unknown wealth to large groups, it tends to more or less completely exclude other groups, which are not needed even for exploitation.[10] Many of us have seen symbolical illustrations on television, in the grotesque images of bodies floating ashore on the coastlines of Southern Europe, primarily black bodies, bodies of people who have not been able to find a living in their African home countries and have hoped for a new life in a wealthy Europe, where they are even less welcome.[11] These are brutal images of

10. Hoogvelt, *Globalisation and the Post-Colonial World*, 239f.
11. The conditions of the boat-refugees from Africa have been investigated by the

the changing reality that challenges traditional European ways of handling welfare.

Other challenges to the welfare systems are connected to changes in patterns of family and gender. The post-war European welfare systems are all to a certain extent built on the idea of stable heterosexual families, with male breadwinners earning the money to support their wives and kids, but even more with wives, grand-mothers, mothers-in-law, sisters and daughters taking the main responsibility for the caring of kids and dependent adults.[12] Today, the cornerstone constituted by this ordering of family life is threatened. Even in Southern Europe, women are entering the labor market in increasing numbers and in doing so many have to choose between having kids and a professional career because no other child-care systems have developed and no similar change has occurred in the life course of men. Men have not become caregivers to the same degree as women have developed professional careers. Women in Europe are, in fact, twice as likely as men to be involved in providing unpaid child care, as well as caring for ill or elderly adults.[13]

As Monique Kremer points out in a recent book, *How Welfare States Care,* the EU Lisbon agreement set out targets for an increase in female workforce participation, but the presence of these targets is matched by the absence of targets for male participation in care. The presupposition that care is women's work seems still to hold Europe in a tight grip. Kremer argues, however, that if women are to work more away from home, the obvious complement will have to be that men are required to work less in order to have more time to participate in care.[14]

Still, it is the demands from the labor market that dictate much of ongoing changes with regard to family life. The labor market is making new demands on people to be flexible, also geographically. Meanwhile, longer lifespans and changing ideals introduce serial marriages and new constructions of families. Many of these changes are no doubt liberating for the people involved, but still they challenge the dependence on women's care-giving as a key factor in the organization of welfare in Europe.

Italian journalist Fabrizio Gatti who took on the appearance of a refugee and shared their conditions for some time. See Gatti, *Bilal. Viaggiare, lavorare, morire da clandestini.*

12. Morgan, *Working Mothers and the Welfare State*, 70.

13. Daly and Rake, *Gender and the Welfare State*, 55.

14. Kremer, *How Welfare States Care*, 254.

Beyond the quite visible challenges I have described there are, however more subtle changes that have to do with changing cultural values. The US scholar Arlie Russell Hochschild pointed more than a decade ago to the problem of an increasing 'care deficit', a gap in resources needed for a dignified life for those who are dependent on other human beings in their daily life.[15] Strange as it may seem from a neo-liberal ideal of the autonomy of each individual, this dependence on the care of others includes each one of us, even if some of us will have to spend much longer than others in this predicament.

More recently, British scholars Mary Daly and Katherine Rake have made observations similar to Hochschild's in a European context, observing that 'the demand for care is growing at the same time as the supply of private care within the family is contracting'.[16] As Hochschild points out, the care deficit is a cultural problem, closely related to the idealizing of the free and independent individual. Daly and Rake warn that welfare needs are increasingly seen as a responsibility that has to be taken by each individual in the form of private insurance, flexibility on the labor market, life-long learning etc. Welfare in Europe is increasingly individualized.[17]

The hidden truth is, however, that this individualization and the norm of the independent individual still rest on the existence of invisible hands reaching out to those who cannot live up to the ideal. The hidden truth is that these hands most often are the hands of women. The hidden truth, furthermore, is that the work done by these hands is seldom professionalized; it is poorly paid and deemed to be of low status.[18]

Here we approach the issue that is really at stake when we talk about the sake of the world in relation to welfare. It has to do with anthropology, with the view of human beings. Do human beings have an inherent value, related to their very existence, not to their usefulness in the global market economy? Do human beings have a value when they do not produce, when they are dependent, when they are in need of care? And does this caring have a value as an equally deep expression of what it is to be human? Is there even something sacred about this caring for the neediest? That is what the sake of the world is about, with regard to

---

15. Hochshild, "The Culture of Politics."
16. Daly and Rake, *Gender and the Welfare State*, 168.
17. Daly and Rake, *Gender and the Welfare State*, 168–71.
18. Pfau-Effinger and Geissler, *Care and Social Integration*, 5.

the organization of welfare in a late-modern world increasingly left to the laws of the market.

CHURCHES AS SOCIAL AGENTS

The problem is anthropological. It is related to the role of religion in late-modern society, but also to gender and to heteronormative ideals of a nuclear family with a female care giver. It is to this complex relation between gender and the role of religion in ongoing social change that we will now turn our attention.

The results from the Welfare and Religion Project show how the present challenges to European post-war models of welfare organization have given rise to a renewed interest in the role of the churches as providers of social care. This renewed interest in the role of the churches may be explained as a consequence of society's general process of functional differentiation, driven by the principle of rationalization and division of labor. As a consequence of this general change, European majority churches increasingly take on specialized functions in society, along with other specialized actors.[19]

From the viewpoint of nation-states, the European majority churches are attractive as providers of welfare services for several reasons:

- Firstly they have financial and institutional resources and more so than possibly all other agents. As shown in our studies, the European majority churches are normally the major organizations second to the state in the respective country.

- Secondly they have access to a religiously motivated and cheep (female) workforce. As with the labor market in general, the type of labor varies, from unpaid volunteers to paid professionals, but still it is a workforce which most often has a deeper motivation than monthly pay.

- Thirdly the churches have, as far as we have seen in our interviews and in surveys we have come across in the respective countries, high credibility among the populations, at least in the social field. The churches meet huge expectations—on the practical level of providing services as well as on a more value-

---

19. For a development of this statement see Pettersson, "Majority Churches."

based level—of defending values of solidarity and care. Ninety percent of the population in the Swedish case study regarded it as an important task for the church to visit people who are lonely or ill and to help weak and vulnerable groups in society, whereas only eight percent regarded worship services as something important.[20]

- Fourthly the churches have theologically motivated values to defend and act upon, which make them likely to stay with their mission. They will not run to another field of action as soon as more money is likely to be made there, as other private agents are likely to do.

The ecclesiological issues of course concern how the churches shall respond to this interest. The first point to make is maybe that acting for the sake of the world; acting in defense of the little ones; acting out of love for the neighbor, belongs to the church's basic mission.[21] It belongs to the basic mission of Christ and thus has its roots in the Eucharist and the sharing of the one bread that is the body of Christ. There is therefore every reason for the church to be happy when a representative of Swedish public authorities says, interviewed in the Swedish case study, that she expects the church to "represent the basic message that people have to take care of one another."[22]

The question for the churches concerns how to respond to this confidence and the alternatives are of course multiple. The social mission of the European majority churches includes soup kitchens and hostels, homes for elderly and meeting spaces for young people. It includes solidarity between individuals in the workplace, in the neighborhood or at school. But it also includes international solidarity, including fundraising and demonstrations. It consists in writing articles in the newspapers or engaging in a political party. What from a theological point of view is decisive is that the activities are anchored in liturgy, that they have their roots in the biblical stories, that they are consequences of Eucharistic

20. Undersökning om kyrka och välfärd i Gävle år 2005 [Enquiry about church and welfare in Gävle 2005], (unpublished).

21. For a development of the theological arguments along this line from the churches involved in the Welfare and Religion-Project see Ekstrand, "Theological Perspective."

22. Edgardh Beckman et al., "Church of Sweden," 48.

sharing and that they are informed and corrected by the common life of the Christian assembly.

These are necessary theological correctives against the risks that are also involved; one major risk being that the social agency of the church simply makes it easier for society at large to continue down the line towards greater efficiency, better competitive capacity and a reduced view of the human being as only interested in increased consumption. Or the result might be the attitude that I have myself met in a public debate, namely that the churches could be counted on "take care of those who do not fit in" with the ideals of efficiency that increasingly permeate society. To the extent that the churches accept that as a more principal role in society, it may easily legitimate the development towards a society more and more streamlined towards profitability, quite the contrary to what the Swedish interviewee hoped for. For European majority-churches threatened by decreasing membership and financial contributions expanded roles as deliverers of social services may seem like a good option. But if the churches become too dependent on assignments from the authorities for their survival and credibility, that may incapacitate their independent theological judgment.[23]

In Sweden this is a problem more generally discussed among civil society actors. But the risk might be of special importance for the Nordic folk churches as they are closely connected through a million different links with society at large and thus are directly influenced on several levels by ongoing social change. When the church becomes more involved in welfare provision, it may adapt to its new role in the professionalized service economy to the extent that the values that could fill a prophetic function are instead pushed back in the church itself and functional differentiation begins to organize even the internal life of the church. One effect might be that the social role of the church is increasingly separated from the rest of church life.

The risks may be illustrated again by an example taken from the Swedish case study. In the city of Gävle, a Church of Sweden parish is involved in the recently established Family Centre in a part of town (Andersberg) with a disproportionate share of immigrants and people with low income. The centre is run by various public agencies in col-

---

23. For a development of the risks involved in this in the German Protestant situation see Leis-Peters, "The German dilemma."

laboration with the church, which provides the services of a deacon and a church-employed preschool teacher, both women by the way, as are all the personnel at the centre. The collaboration builds on the agreement that the people employed by the church shall be there, not as religious representatives, but as social professionals. The parish has agreed to this, because it will still be able to serve a social need. But it is also the case that Church of Sweden parish was previously present in Andersberg by way of a district church. When other public services left Andersberg, the church building was sold too. The previous liturgical presence of the church was then replaced with a presence at the Family Centre, based solely on the role as social actor.[24]

The example illustrates the pressure put on churches in a specialized society not to so to speak "mix" their social involvement with too much "religion." The social agency has to remain social and not become an arena for evangelization. But then, we may ask from an ecclesiological perspective, what happens if the church's social work, its care for the needy and poor that it may encounter at the Family Centre, loses its anchorage in the Eucharist and the thanksgiving for the gifts of God in Jesus? On the other hand, what happens to the celebration of the Eucharist if it loses its relation to the needs of the world, to the real needs of the real people who come to the Family Centre?

FUNCTIONAL DIFFERENTIATION AND GENDER

Separation of social action from liturgical life may easily be underpinned by the gender divide pointed to above. Church social work all over Europe is primarily carried out by women, at the same time as women are much less well represented in positions of leadership and the ordained ministry that is responsible for the liturgical life of the churches. This is not only the case in the Catholic and Orthodox churches, where women are by definition excluded from the ordained ministry. The situation is quite similar in Sweden, a country that is often seen as a herald of gender equality and where the Lutheran church is officially committed to the aim of equality between women and men. Certainly the fact that for 50 years now, women are ordained as priests in the Swedish church does make a difference, but it is more the case, as in other parts of working life, that even if women slowly make their way into the traditional male domains,

24. Edgardh and Pettersson, "Report."

men are very slow to take up traditionally female roles. As an example, only about 13 percent of the deacons, who normally are the officials who are responsible for the social work in Swedish parishes, are men, and only 21 percent of the vicars, who are responsible for the worship life of the parishes, are women.[25]

This gender divide in turn seems to be a major factor being the broader population's distrust of the churches. The qualitative interviews carried out in the Welfare and Religion Project contained numerous spontaneous negative comments about the attitude of the churches to issues of gender, family and sexuality. A quote from a young male Finnish interviewee may illustrate, as he says that "All these discussions on women priests and gays and stuff, it really is quite depressing to listen—it is like gosh, we have already moved on from the days when grandpa bought his first watch—don't they get it?"[26]

Quotes like this illustrate on the local level the conflicts around issues of gender, family and sexuality that receive so much attention in media.[27] This kind of suspicious attitude to the churches from Europeans seems, however, not to prevent female gendering of social care work from being taken as something very natural. This is true for Europe more generally, but is also a clearly visible tendency in the case studies of the Welfare and Religion Project. Irrespective of the context, interviewees representing churches, public authorities and local population tended to take for granted that care is a female responsibility, and often also a natural consequence of supposedly natural traits related to gender. Some quotes may illustrate: "Diaconal activities are care work; typically women things" states a Norwegian interviewee.[28] "[Women] are more predisposed to care giving," an Italian interviewee fills in.[29] "The woman is more familiar with this type of work" echoes a Greek interviewee.[30]

---

25. "Jämställdheten i Svenska kyrkan." [Gender Equality in the Church of Sweden].

26. Yeung, "Finnish Lutheran Church," 194.

27. For a development of this argument, see Edgardh, "Analysis from a Gender Perspective."

28. Angell and Wyller, "Church of Norway," 122.

29. Frisina, "Catholic Church in Italy," 200.

30. Fokas, "Greek Orthodox Church," 248.

GENDER COMPLEMENTARITY

In some churches, the Roman-Catholic and the Greek Orthodox in particular, this female gendering of care is underpinned by official statements about the complementary roles of women and men. These are in turn sometimes reinforced by references to Mary, the mother of Jesus, being held forth as a role model for women. As it is said in a "Letter to the Bishops" from the Vatican Congregation of Faith in 2004 "Women are called to be unique examples and witnesses for all Christians of how the Bride is to respond in love to the love of the Bridegroom." To illustrate ideal femininity is however not the original or deepest theological function of Mariology. Thus the Vatican tries to keep together a supposedly given complementarity of male and female gender with presenting Mary as a role model for both women and men. In another part of the letter it is underlined that " . . . the feminine values mentioned here are above all human values: the human condition of man and woman created in the image of God is one and indivisible." The Vatican takes pains about explaining this complicated understanding of a femininity that is a humanity, while still somehow more limited to femininity anyhow. The paragraph thus continues:

> It is only because women are more immediately attuned to these values that they are the reminder and the privileged sign of such values. But, in the final analysis, every human being, man or woman, is destined to be "for the other". In this perspective, that which is called "femininity" is more than simply an attribute of the female sex. The word designates indeed the fundamental human capacity to live for the other and because of the other.[31]

The tendency to restrict the role of Mary to that of a role model for women is however not limited to the Catholic and Orthodox traditions. The role of Mary in the spiritual life of Church of Sweden was greatly diminished by the Reformation and especially so during the period of the Lutheran Orthodoxy. Even so Mary as a model, not for the Church or for humanity, but for women, seems to flourish at least as well in the Swedish secular context as in more traditionally religious contexts. An exhibition at the Historical museum in Stockholm 2008–2009 on the theme "Mary—the female ideal" [Maria—drömmen om kvinnan] received a lot of media at-

---

31. Congregation for the doctrine of the faith.

tention. The exhibition was presented as being about Mary as a role model for what it means to be a real woman, according to a secular Swedish newspaper "suffering, praying and perfect"! "Mary is a role model who is constantly topical" said the producer of the exhibition in a quote; "Every day we may see examples in the media of how she influences how women are portrayed."[32]

The exhibition illustrates how Christian imagery, and especially imagery connected to Mary, contributes to closely connect care to femininity even in a highly secular country like Sweden. Associations of this type have been questioned for decades by feminist theologians, but the most basic challenge still remains, namely to reevaluate serving and care as human ideals rather than female. As long as the Christian arguments are caught in a simultaneous devaluation of women and an idealization of caring as a specific feminine quality the prospects of succeeding seem bleak. Not even feminist theology is sufficiently equipped for meeting the challenge, to the extent that it too is caught in the very same conceptualization of a basic gender division in society. It is exactly at this point that queer theology might offer better, or at least complementary, tools.

Feminist theology has been characterized by a strong commitment to justice and solidarity, explicitly critical of patriarchal church traditions and demanding access to their privileged male dominated arenas. But that is very far from where most of the women who are given a voice in the studies of the Welfare and Religion Project find themselves, or would even like to be. Many, probably a majority, of the women involved in the social work of the European churches are quite content to not be invited into any church hierarchies. Rather they find meaning and satisfaction in their lives through caring for others. The social work as a separate sphere allows its contributors a degree of independence and offers them a feeling of importance. The women involved may, as formulated in the Greek case study report,

> express a sense of pride in their work . . . welfare activity is considered important, and their service to people in need is . . . an important role that they can play within the Church. In this sense, women working within Church welfare services may be consid-

---

32. Dagens Nyheter 8 August, 2008.

ered to be functioning as if they were deaconesses ... without any resentment that they are not official, ordained deaconesses ... [33]

If feminist theology is best summarized in the word justice, the work of these women is rather about caring and serving; these two poles do not easily interact, as has been much discussed in feminist ethics in recent decades. From a justice point of view, the very idea that some women voluntarily want to serve, with neither payment nor substantial influence on decision-making, is quite provocative. It seems that these women do not want to be liberated in the way that feminism has envisioned. This may be one explanation why few feminist theologians have engaged with the reality where women are a majority, as in church-related social work, but instead have focused on claiming access to interpretative authority over liturgy, biblical exegesis or dogmatics, i.e. to the centers of power in church hierarchies.

This has definitely been a very important contribution. But it is not enough, as long as it leaves the problems of gender connected to the reality documented in the Welfare and Religion Project intact. What is needed is a theology where the feminist claims for justice are integrated with the values upheld by women and men engaged in social practices. Together, these two aspects may serve as building blocks for realizing an alternative theopolitical vision, characterized by guarding basic values of care and solidarity that are under increasing pressure and threat in the world of today, a theopolitical vision that in the words of the feminist ethicist Virginia Held would encourage European societies to "begin to think about how society should be reorganized to be hospitable to care, rather than continuing to marginalize it."[34]

Most researchers on welfare and gender agree that such a social change would have to involve deep structural changes not only in the lives of women, but also in the lives of men, who would have to take a much more active role in the care of their fellow human beings than they do at present and thus probably also allow more vulnerability to be part of their daily life. This is also what leading experts on the organization of welfare in Europe argue for. Along with several of his colleagues among welfare researchers, the Danish scholar Gøsta Esping-Andersen argues that the only way forward for the European welfare states is that a similar change

33. Fokas, "Greek Orthodox Church," 260f.
34. Held, *Ethics of Care*, 18.

takes place in the life-course of men to that which has already happened to women. As women have in recent decades increasingly become breadwinners along with men, so men have to become care-givers along with women if the welfare of present and future generations is to be secured.[35]

THE QUEER CONTRIBUTION

The European majority churches will have great problems contributing to European social politics along this line, without a basic revision of their ideologies and practices related to gender, family and sexuality. These ideologies and practices are today securely founded on assumptions of gender complementarity, heteronormativity and female responsibility for caring. In that situation it seems totally utopian to envision that the European majority churches will take part in a more prophetic mission of defending values of care and solidarity as Christian visions for humanity, rather than protecting continued dependence on women's more or less voluntary serving under the umbrella of the traditional nuclear family. But it is exactly at this point I think queer theology might provide a creative impulse that could take the churches a bit further, further even than what feminist theology has so far been able to do.

The interesting theological question raised by the authors of *Queer Theology* is to what extent the values defended by conservative forces in the churches really are "Christian" and in what sense they may be claimed as "tradition." Several of the authors engage in a rereading of tradition, a queer reading that invites us to reevaluate things we take for granted. Most contemporary debates concerning family and sexuality, for example, start from the presupposition that the churches have always advocated heterosexual family life. Even radical debaters most often accept these assumptions, even if they argue that the churches have the right to reevaluate their ideals when society changes. The authors of *Queer theology,* however, reject the assumption as such. Instead they argue, primarily by way of various genealogical studies, that the very idea of two distinct sexes, of heterosexual attraction as the only normal attraction, and of the nuclear family as the only right way of living this attraction, and even more as the basis for divided gender roles, are quite late phenomena in the history of the Western world and thus also in the history of the Western churches. In fact, they show, these ideals are to a large extent the result of needs

35. Esping-Andersen, *Why We Need a New Welfare State*, 70.

that have developed in the modernizing period from the 16th century onwards.[36]

In a similar vein, the Norwegian New Testament scholar Jorunn Økland has questioned the idea that the nuclear family has a normative anchorage in the biblical canon. Christian arguments in defense of the nuclear family are rather arguments in favor of an imitation of an original that does not exist, she says, but an original that these arguments construct as a model and read into the biblical text.[37]

As a result of this type of rereading, conservative forces that claim to speak out as guardians of values of solidarity and care rooted in the teachings of Jesus and the Apostles, rather appear as guardians of specific family patterns developed during recent centuries in Western Europe. As Elisabeth Stuart argues in *Queer Theology*, "the Western churches currently give every impression of wanting to produce heterosexual desire rather than desire for God . . . "[38]

BACK TO THE FUTURE

To the extent that the Christian churches dare to take a step back from present practices and debates, they might rediscover unique resources for envisioning multiple forms of human community-building in their own traditions, for example in the history of religious sister- and brotherhoods. Such queer dimensions of church traditions might help to redirect the interest of the church leaders from the struggle to uphold heterosexual desire and modern, or even post Second World War patterns of family life, to a reorienting of theology to deal with the human desire for God and the teachings of Jesus on serving and care for the neighbor.

What queer theology might thus contribute is not primarily inspiration from recent trends in academic studies on gender and sexuality, but inspiration from within the Christian traditions themselves, that might question contemporary convictions around sexual difference, sexual desires and reproduction, or as Gerard Loughlin writes in his introduction to *Queer Theology* " . . . the point is not to queer the tradition, but to let its orientation queer us."[39]

36. Shaw, "Reformed and Enlightened" and Woodhead, "Sex and Secularisation."
37. Økland, "Du skall ikke."
38. Stuart, "Sacramental Flesh," 70.
39. Loughlin, "Introduction: The End of Sex," 12.

What Loughlin and others invite us to do is to return to tradition, not in order to go back—feminist theology has shown the destructive potentials of that—but to carry us into the future, to seek arguments to question some of the cornerstones on which much of the social agency of the churches today are built. Queer theologians encourage Christian traditions to question the nuclear family as the deepest Christian calling; to question desire for the other sex as the deepest human desire; and even to question sexual identity as the deepest human identity.

With our eyes cleared by these deconstructions, we might even be able to return to Mary in her secular captivity at the exhibition in Stockholm, in order to free her from the contemporary ideals of femininity in which she seems to be completely bound up. Freed from these ideals, she may rise at our side as a role model, not for women, but for Christian discipleship, a model for both men and women in being church—in the deepest sense being human—together.

For this endeavor, great resources might be found in Eastern as well as Western church traditions. Downplayed as these queer resources may be in present church life, they could be developed to offer men and women alternative platforms for caring for each other and for raising their voices for justice and social change. To the extent that this is fulfilled, the churches may find a prophetic mission deeply anchored in the gospel *and* desperately needed in a secular post-industrial Europe where values associated with serving, mutuality, solidarity, patience and vulnerability are increasingly out of mode.

BIBLIOGRAPHY

Angell, Olav Helge and Trygve Wyller. "The Church of Norway as an Agent of Welfare—the case of Drammen." In *Churches in Europe as Agents of Welfare—Sweden, Norway and Finland*, edited by Anne Yeung et al., 86–141. Working Paper 2:1 from the project Welfare and Religion in a European Perspective. Diakonivetenskapliga institutets skriftserie 11. Uppsala: DVI, 2006.

Berger, Peter, et al. *Religious America, Secular Europe. A Theme and Variations*. Aldershot: Ashgate, 2008.

Bäckström, Anders, et al. *Welfare and Religion in 21st Century Europe: Volume 1. Configuring the Connections*. Aldershot: Ashgate (forthcoming).

Bäckström, Anders, et al. *Welfare and Religion in 21st Century Europe: Volume 2. Gendered, Religious and Social Change*. Aldershot: Ashgate, (forthcoming).

Congregation for the doctrine of the faith. "Letter to the Bishops of the Catholic Church on the collaboration of men and women in the Church and in the world." 31 July

2004. No pages. Online: http://www.vatican.va/roman_curia/congregations/cfaith/documents/rc_con_cfaith_doc_20040731_collaboration_en.html.

Dagens Nyheter, 8 August (2008). "Maria och mode på museer." Kulturdelen, 5.

Daly, Mary and Katherine Rake. *Gender and the Welfare State. Care, Work and Welfare in Europe and the USA*. Cambridge: Polity Press, 2003.

Edgardh, Ninna, "Analysis from a Gender Perspective." In *Welfare and Religion in 21st Century Europe: Volume 2. Gendered, Religious and Social Change*, edited by Anders Bäckström et al. Aldershot: Ashgate, (forthcoming).

Edgardh, Ninna, and Per Pettersson. "Report from the Swedish case study within the European Commission 6th framework project *Welfare and Values in Europe. Transitions related to Religion, Minorities and Gender,*" 2007. Online: http://www.waveproject.org/output/Case_Study_Reports/D9_-_Gavle.pdf.

Edgardh Beckman, Ninna et. al. "The Church of Sweden as an Agent of Welfare. The Case of Gävle." In *Churches in Europe as Agents of Welfare—Sweden, Norway and Finland*, edited by Anne Yeung et al., 20–85. Working Paper 2:1 from the project Welfare and Religion in a European Perspective. Diakonivetenskapliga institutets skriftserie 11. Uppsala: DVI, 2006.

Ekstrand, Thomas. "A Theological Perspective on Churches as Agents of Welfare." In *Welfare and Religion in 21st Century Europe: Volume 2. Gendered, Religious and Social Change*, edited by Anders Bäckström et al. Aldershot: Ashgate, (forthcoming).

Esping-Andersen, Gøsta. *Why We Need a New Welfare State*. Oxford: Oxford University Press, 2002.

Fokas, Effie. "The Greek Orthodox Church as an Agent of Welfare—the case of Thiva and Livadeia." In *Churches in Europe as Agents of Welfare—England, Germany, France, Italy and Greece*, edited by Anne Yeung et al., 218–64. Working Paper 2:2 from the project Welfare and Religion in a European Perspective. Diakonivetenskapliga institutets skriftserie 12. Uppsala: DVI, 2006.

Frisina, Annalisa. "The Catholic Church in Italy as an Agent of Welfare—the case of Vicenza." In *Churches in Europe as Agents of Welfare—England, Germany, France, Italy and Greece*, edited by Anne Yeung et al., 182–217. Working Paper 2:2 from the project Welfare and Religion in a European Perspective. Diakonivetenskapliga institutets skriftserie 12. Uppsala: DVI, 2006.

Gatti, Fabrizio. *Bilal. Viaggiare, lavorare, morire da clandestini*. Milano: Rizzoli/BUR, 2008.

Held, Virginia. *The Ethics of Care. Personal, Political, Global*. New York: Oxford University Press, 2006.

Hochschild, Arlie Russell. "The Culture of Politics. Traditional, Postmodern, Cold-modern, and Warm-modern Ideals of Care." *Social Politics* (Fall 1995). Volume 2:3, 331–46.

Hoogvelt, Anki. *Globalisation and the Post-Colonial World. The New Political Economy of Development*. London: Macmillan Press, 1997.

"Jämställdheten i Svenska kyrkan" [Gender Equality in Church of Sweden]. Missive to the Church Synod 2008. Kyrkomötet, Kyrkostyrelsens skrivelse 2008:6, June 13 (2008). Online: http://www.svenskakyrkan.se/tcrot/km/2008/skrivelser/KsSkr%20 2008_06%20Jämställdhet.shtml#TopOfPage.

Kremer, Monique. *How Welfare States Care: Culture, Gender and Parenting in Europe*. Amsterdam: Amsterdam University Press, 2007.

Leis-Peters, Annette. "The German dilemma—Protestant agents of welfare in Reutlingen." In *Welfare and Religion in 21st century Europe: Volume 1. Re-configuring the Connections*, edited by Anders Bäckström and Grace Davie. Aldershot: Ashgate (forthcoming).

Loughlin, Gerard. "Introduction: The End of Sex." In *Queer Theology. Rethinking the Western Body*, edited by Gerard Loughlin. Oxford: Blackwell 2007.

Loughlin, Gerard. *Queer Theology. Rethinking the Western Body*, Oxford: Blackwell, 2007.

Morgan, Kimberly J. *Working Mothers and the Welfare State. Religion and Politics of Work-Family Policies in Western Europe and the United States*. Stanford: Stanford University Press, 2006.

Pettersson, Per. "Majority Churches as European Welfare Agents—A Sociological Analysis at Three Levels." In *Welfare and Religion in 21st Century Europe: Volume 2. Gendered, Religious and Social Change*, edited by Anders Bäckström et al. Aldershot: Ashgate, (forthcoming).

Pfau-Effinger, Birgit, and Birgit Geissler. *Care and Social Integration in European Societies*. Bristol: Policy Press, 2005.

Shaw, Jane. "Reformed and Enlightened Church." In *Queer Theology. Rethinking the Western Body*, edited by Gerard Loughlin, 215-29. Oxford: Blackwell, 2007.

Stuart, Elisabeth. "Sacramental Flesh." In *Queer Theology. Rethinking the Western Body*, edited by Gerard Loughlin, 65-75. Oxford: Blackwell, 2007.

Turner, William Benjamin. *A Genealogy of Queer Theory*. Philadelphia: Temple University Press, 2000.

Undersökning om kyrka och välfärd i Gävle år 2005 [Enquiry about church and welfare in Gävle 2005], (unpublished).

Woodhead, Linda. "Sex and Secularisation." In *Queer Theology. Rethinking the Western Body*, edited by Gerard Loughlin, 230-44. Oxford: Blackwell, 2007.

Yeung, Anne Birgitta. "The Finnish Lutheran Church as an Agent of Welfare—the case of Lahti." In *Churches in Europe as Agents of Welfare—Sweden, Norway and Finland*, edited by Anne Yeung et al., 142-203. Working Paper 2:1 from the project Welfare and Religion in a European Perspective. Diakonivetenskapliga institutets skriftserie 11. DVI: Uppsala, 2006.

Økland, Jorunn. "Du skall ikke imitere ekteskapet. Forestillinger om Den Hellige kjerne-Familie." st. sunniva tidskrift for norsk kvinnelig teologforening, nr 3-4/2006/14. årgang, 115-33.

She Keeps Bothering Me

Human Rights and Suffering

GÖRAN GUNNER

A CRIME AGAINST HUMANITY AND THE IDENTITY OF THE CHURCH

There is an open fireplace and some women dressed in colorful traditional African clothing are preparing the morning tea. Some have already started to work with their pickaxes in a tiny vegetable garden. This could be any African village but next to the women are several hundred other women and young girls standing or sitting on homemade benches. They are all joined together by an outrageous cruelty. They have been brutally raped and exposed to extreme sexual violence by members of armed groups committing their crimes in gangs, but also by army-soldiers and even by fellow villagers. By foot the women have come from villages to the hospital hoping for some physical treatment. But that is not enough—most of them have been stigmatized for lifetime. They have been rejected by husbands, expelled from their families, the village and even from the local church. And even history is frightening. In the early 20th century, Leopold II of Belgium was presiding over a political system in Congo where slave labor caused the death of approximately ten million people.[1] During the last decade, approximately four million more Congolese have been killed. What happens in the eastern part of the Democratic Republic of Congo is according to international law described as a crime against humanity.

1. Hochschild, *King Leopold's Ghost*, 225–34.

However, that does not give any justice to the women who are victims and completely marginalized in society. They cannot go to the state courts since the court system is completely corrupt. If they succeed in bringing the perpetrator to the traditional courts under the mango tree, a so-called peaceful agreement will be made with compensation to the husband or father but with the woman still a rejected victim. Clearly, these violations are not only, maybe not foremost, directed against individuals. The aim is to destroy the society by fragmentizing families, isolating individuals, and breaking down infrastructure and, as a consequence, destroying the social setting. A background document at the Ninth Assembly of the Word Council of Churches in Porto Alegre 2006 states:

> The respect for human dignity and the active promotion of the common good are imperatives of the gospel of Jesus Christ, i.e. persons, men and women, are created in the image of God and justified by grace. Human rights should therefore be emphasized as a basic element of praxis of preventing violence and of shaping a just peace.[2]

Baptism and Eucharist are integral parts of the Christian identity as individuals belong to the church as a community of followers. At the same time, when the church appears in a concrete manner, it is also about relations—relations not only between a human being and God but also between human beings in their daily lives. When dealing with ecclesiology, one way of expressing the church is through the image of "the body of Christ." This image implies that each part of the Body has a responsibility in relation to other parts of the body, since all belong together.

In line with the imperatives of the Gospel, the church's identity involves commitments with the aim of trying to understand what it means to be Christians today. At the heart of the church is the question of how to relate to today's human situation as regards human dignity within the community but involving the whole of humanity as created images of God.

Two traditional ways of expressing the identity of the church are the church as messenger and the church as servant. In this presentation I am

---

2. Mid-term of the Ecumenical Decade to Overcome Violence 2001–2010. Online: http://www.oikoumene.org/en/resources/documents/assembly/porto-alegre-2006/3-preparatory-and-background-documents/mid-term-of-the-ecumenical-decade-to-overcome-violence-2001-2010.html.

going to use the concept of *addressed participants,* indicating a church as a responding community, responding to the Word and responding to the situation in the world.

If the church consists of addressed participants, it would then also be possible to evaluate the church as a responding community, or if you like, as messenger and servant, by the ability to build an inclusive good life for humankind, the vision of the Kingdom of God with justice enabling peace, followed by reconciliation and forgiveness. The image of the church as the Body of Christ gives the idea that everyone is included. Whatever happens to one part is of importance to other parts and to the entirety: "If one part suffers, every part suffers with it; if one part is honored, every part rejoices with it" (1 Cor 12:26). But Christ goes beyond the already addressed participants when in his mission he identifies with the most marginalized, oppressed and suffering individuals in society. Then the identity of the church as addressed participants needs to "go beyond" as a community in solidarity, including people being violated.

HUMAN SUFFERING AND THE GOOD LIFE

Theologians have been working with the challenge of constructing a theology that names human suffering and the longing for a good life rooted in the identity of the church or the body of Christ. This may be done in the setting of formulating a theological anthropology, as Eleazar S. Fernandez in his *Reimagining the Human,* with the conclusion that it is a "process of becoming human" involving "dreaming and acting as if the dreamed for humanity were already a present reality."[3] Or it may be as in George Newlands' *Christ and Human Rights,* aiming at the construction of a Christology which centers on a Christ of the vulnerable and the margins,[4] or in the setting of Christian ecclesiology as William T. Cavanaugh in *Torture and Eucharist.* While torture is considered a kind of perverse liturgy, the Eucharist is the response from the church which:

> [c]reates martyrs out of victims by calling the church to acts of self-sacrifice and remembrance, honouring in Jesus' sacrifice the countless to the conflict between the powers of life and the powers of death. The true "discipline of the secret" calls Christians to

---

3. Fernandez, *Reimagining the Human,* 229.
4. Newlands, *Christ and Human Rights.*

become the true body of Christ, and to bring to light the suffering of others by making that suffering visible in their own bodies.[5]

Through an interpretation of the church as a community in solidarity, a critical analysis of unjust structures is possible. These structures may be found both inside and outside the church, and are causing suffering, destruction, oppression and death to human beings, with crimes against humanity among the most devastating expressions. But here we also find other factors stigmatizing and marginalizing at least parts of the church, as diseases like the HI-virus causing AIDS. Although the pandemic never acts alone but often goes hand in hand with conditions of poverty and gender relations, it is a crisis for the church. Denice M. Ackermann uses the expression "the Body of Christ has AIDS" and states that the Eucharist is connecting over space and time. The Eucharist aims at celebrating and at remembering the violated body of Tamar connected to "the abused bodies of women and children, the bodies of people living with HIV and AIDS and the crucified and resurrected body of Jesus Christ." She writes:

> Deep inside the Body of Christ, the AIDS virus lurks and as we remember Christ's sacrifice, we see in his very wounds the woundedness of his sisters and brothers who are infected and dying.[6]

HUMAN SUFFERING AND HUMAN RIGHTS

It may be argued that at the heart of the church is the duty of restoring human beings who are suffering and have been violated—maybe through torture, maybe HIV, or poverty. Or, taken from another point of view, what should the church do with the abusers, as Miroslav Volf discuss in *The End of Memory*.[7] The identity of the church, the body of Christ, is dependent on the ability to deal with questions of violations, abuses, stigmatization and marginalization.

The church looked upon in this way will have to deal with power and misuse of power, with oppression and injustice, with violence and suffering, with discrimination and marginalization. Finding ways to deal with these kinds of issues is also the business of human rights. I want to suggest that the vision of the Kingdom of God and the vision of human rights

5. Cavanaugh, *Torture and Eucharist*, 281.
6. Ackermann, "Tamar's Cry," 51.
7. Volf, *The End of Memory*.

are very similar in their aspirations. Both aim to include all humankind in the good life. They are both the theological/ideological point of departure and the final goal. They include ideas about how to analyze the current situation at the same time as they are instruments for implementation.

In this presentation, I am not interested in arguments to legitimize either a dissociation or the opposite between the church and human rights, but I want to look into an assumed existing relation. My assumption is that interdependence exists between human rights advocacy and the church understood as a community of addressed participants. Highlighting this relation may help the church as addressed participants to be more faithful and responsive as part and parcel of its identity. I am aware this approach may be seen as asking the church to subscribe to the myth of human rights as a saviour but my question is rather if human rights may be said to interrelate to an inclusive identity of the church as the body of Christ. And that especially when states and authorities fail to protect human beings as individuals and as members of communities or when states even take part in ongoing violations and human rights abuse. So, I want to use parts of the discussion about the human rights discourse to challenge the church to visibility.

ON HUMAN RIGHTS AND THE STATE

Human rights are a body of laws, of legal documents, founded on the principle of the inherent dignity of the human being, recognizing the rights of all human beings to freedom, justice, and non-discrimination. As such, agreed to by states, including a will to implement and improve the rights, they may be considered as a framework, even though not all conventions have been ratified by all states. In principle, the agreed rights imply that each and every person has the same rights in relation to the state and should be protected against state abuse and excess of power, besides being protected against abuse performed by other actors in society. These rights are claimed to be universal, indivisible, interdependent and interrelated.[8] Human rights may be looked upon as the agreed consensus on a minimum standard for everyone to enjoy a life in dignity, but also as a dynamic framework involved in a process of interpretation in situations with current violations and as yet unfulfilled rights.

---

8. Vienna declaration 1993 (section I§5).

Yes, I know, there are dilemmas and severe problems. Human rights violations seem still to be the norm in many countries. In one way it is a failure by the state but most of all for the individual calling day and night for justice. Sometimes states, for better but usually for worse, reject the concept of human rights, talking about "national and regional particularities and various historical, cultural and religious backgrounds."[9] Such an approach prompts me to ask: In whose interest? Since often it is about preserving traditional privileges and power structures. According to the human rights concept, the states of the world are considered to be of good will and in favor of implementing rights for their people. Yet, we know it is not always that easy since there is still human vulnerability, discrimination, misuse of power and unequal distribution of resources. But still, there is no other alternative, universally trying to protect us as human beings.

The human rights system is calculating alternative options in cases where a certain state seems not to bother about performing violations against its people. The "mobilization of shame" model, exposing violations of human rights, presupposes that international political and moral pressure produces results. Another argument is that international pressure is needed because people locally seem to lack opportunities for protection of their rights.

Today, responsibility for human rights, primarily as a relation between the nation-state and the individual, is questioned. That is not the same as questioning human rights as such, or questioning the need of legal implementation; it is to question the state as the sole actor with the individual as an isolated counterparty. The church as a body of addressed participants does have a special duty to take responsibility in this situation.

SHE KEEPS BOTHERING ME

My doctoral training in theology started in the field of New Testament studies with the aim of producing a thesis about the parables in Luke. The project was never completed because I changed disciplines and started to work on the history of religion. However, since then I do have a predilection for the parables and cannot resist reading one of them in this context. Kenneth E. Bailey interpreted not just the parables in Luke but the com-

9. Bangkok Governmental Declaration 1993.

position of the texts in Luke, using chiasms and literary structures built on parallelism, starting simultaneously from the beginning and the end of a specific text. In this way he ended up in the centre of the text where he found an important aspect of its message.[10] I will apply his model of inverted parallelism to Luke 18:1–8, starting simultaneously with verse 1 and verse 8.

In Luke 17, in the context of an eschatological discussion, Jesus is talking to his disciples about his suffering and the coming of the days of the Son of Man. He is asked about the Kingdom of God gives the disciples an answer about his coming suffering, accompanied by a parable.

The introduction in 18:1 is a request by Jesus to the disciples to pray and not give up. Verse 8 concludes with a question as to whether the coming Son of Man will find faith on Earth, thereby connecting the present with the future. I am aware there are no little debate about what belongs to the parable proper, what its focus is, and what sort of image of God is proposed to the reader. Luke's framework of the text easily invites an interpretation that it is all about spirituality—Jesus, as already in verse 1, is recommending persistent faith-inspired prayer to God as a mode of Christian life.[11] I have no problem with that but will read the entire text as if the example not accidentally but purposefully includes a message, especially against the background of widows as a vulnerable group in the Bible. My intention is not to allegorize but to use the text as projecting meaning in new situations. The reader will for sure think about what is happening to the widow and the judge.

A judge in a local city appears not to fear God and, most important, not to care about human beings. Not prepared to give the widow her right, he is an abuser, a man violating the right of a human being. In contrast, the text states that God will intervene with justice and do so quickly instead of waiting for the end and the coming of the Son of Man.

There is a widow in the local city, an individual presenting a plea to be granted justice. If the parallelism works, she is related to God's chosen ones. An individual claiming a human right is part of the group crying

---

10. Bailey, *Poet & Peasant*, 48.

11. See as an example: Fitzmyer, *The Gospel According to Luke*, 1175–78. Bernard Brandon Scott says that the "parable itself functions as an example based on 'how much more': if an unjust judge grants a widow her petition because of constant intercession, how much more will God." See Scott, *Hear Then the Parable*, 176.

She Keeps Bothering Me

day and night for justice. She appears as an individual voice, but at the same time represents all individuals being violated.

The abuser sticks to his refusal but the Lord knows that even when being unjust, the judge is not unimpressionable.

She keeps on bothering and that will wear him out. It seems that the necessary task at hand is to be troublesome. Nagging by one individual is parallel and inseparable from the group of chosen ones—crying day and night. Do not give up, keep on bothering, wearing them out. The victim's world is the world of the chosen ones and thereby the world of the church.

In the centre of the text, the parallel structure points to a kind of conclusion: justice will be granted (*ekdikēsō autēn*). It seems that at this point, God and the judge coincide and at that moment the widow will be granted justice and the crying out by the chosen ones successful. He will not put them off.

18:1. Jesus pray and not give up	18:8. The Son of Man will he find faith
2. a judge neither feared God nor cared about men	God he will see that they get justice, and quickly
3. a widow kept coming to him with the plea Grant me justice	7. his chosen ones cry out to him day and night Will he keep putting them off?
4. (judge) he refused I don't fear God or care about men	6. the Lord said Listen to what the unjust judge says
5. this widow keeps bothering me	eventually wears me out with her coming
I will see that she gets justice	

"I will see that she gets justice" and to achieve this there may be a need for quite a lot of bothering, of crying out day and night for those in power to take action against perpetrators. And the individual is never alone. Whether or not the chosen ones have the same experience, they are united in one body and are acting as a voice on behalf of the suffering part of the body. And not just as a voice but as a determined lobby-group never giving up. As to the question at the end of the text: if the Son of Man will find faith, that maybe include not only faith in God, in the Trinity and so on, but also in a faithful bothering and wearing out of authorities, in whatever shape they take. A faithful nagging about justice on earth. Will there be any "addressed participants" left? Will the church be faithful in crying out and including the suffering part of the body of Christ?

CHURCH PRIORITIES AND A HUMAN RIGHTS-LANGUAGE

It is necessary for the church as addressed participant to have an identity, centered around the Eucharist, Baptism and the Word, to rejoice when one part is honored. But it is also necessary to find appropriate methods and instruments to analyze relations and situations where a part is suffering. In human life, those situations are often characterized by violation, abuse, stigmatization, and marginalization. If the church wants to be a messenger and a servant, she needs to be equipped with tools for challenging these situations and being instrumental for change.

At least some parts of the global church-hierarchies consider that one way of dealing with these questions is through the human rights-agenda.[12] That does not mean that that is the only way or that the church should become a human rights organization. But it is to agree with Charles Villa-Vicencio, who declares:

> To the extent that it provides a basis for ideological critique, while contributing to a better understanding of humanity, as a basis for the promotion of such rights that sustain human dignity, a theological silence in the face of human rights violations can only be constructed as morally repugnant and socially irresponsible. . . . The task of theology is to help locate the human rights struggle at the centre of the debate on what it means to be human and therefore also at the centre of social and political pursuit.[13]

The language of human rights may enable the church as the body of Christ to create an inclusive identity, taking violated people into account. And it seems that the language of a human rights-based approach is close to the Christian language since it is about human dignity and human suffering.

In order to keep this identity in the "centre," it is necessary to involve the "periphery." The Pakistani theologian Charles Amjad-Ali has reflected about passion for change, when reading the Gospel of Mark:

12. See Jacques, *Resisting the Intolerable*.
13. Villa-Vicencio, "Theology and Human Rights."

> I think it is very clear from the evidence that Jesus was seen as subverting the whole socio-political and economic order by bringing the people who were pushed onto the outside of society into the very centre of things. Further, having rehabilitated a person from the periphery to the centre, Jesus himself is pushed out to the periphery, so that he "had to stay outside in places where nobody lived". Even here, at the periphery, "people from all around would come to him" (1:45). Here I think the full implication of Heb 13:12–14 becomes fully manifested, because it is stated that "and so Jesus too suffered outside the gate to sanctify the people with his own blood. Let us go to him, then *outside the camp*, and share his degradation." This passage from Hebrews not only states where Jesus was located but also makes a similar demand on those who are his follower.[14]

Here the identity of the church is associated with its ability to take into account the so-called periphery and people at the border. In biblical language that may mean to cross human borders, such as Samaria, Syrian Phoenicia or even enter the dark corners of the Gerasenes. Being outside the camp is to include the most discriminated or violated human beings, each one created as an image of God. Without enabling a capacity that includes the periphery, the church will have problems identifying with the image of being the body of Christ. In a human rights-based approach it is possible to find the same focus. Among other thing, there is a need of mainstreaming, always putting:

- an emphasis on the poorest, the most marginalized and the most vulnerable in society (which often means women and children)
- an emphasis on gender perspectives as well as focusing on gender equality
- an emphasis on non-discrimination
- an emphasis on groups of people who are discriminated against because of HIV-status, lacking financial resources, ethnic belonging, disablement, sex, age etc.

There is in the human rights-based approach a stress on the need of transparency, accountability and the rule of law but also a need of culpability,

---

14. Amjad-Ali, *Passion for Change*, 16–17.

in the sense that anyone violating human rights should be held responsible for what has happened and justice be done.

It is easy to find biblical quotations, more or less like well-known slogans, with the same intention as found in a human rights-based approach, like:

> The Spirit of the Lord is on me, because he has anointed me to preach good news to the poor. He has sent me to proclaim freedom for the prisoners and recovery of sight for the blind, to release the oppressed (Luke 4:18);

> There is neither Jew nor Greek, slave nor free, male nor female, for you are all one in Christ Jesus (Gal 3:28);

> So in everything, do to others what you would have them do to you, for this sums up the Law and the Prophets (Matt 7:12);

> Love your neighbor as yourself (Matt 22:39);

> Selling their possessions and goods, they gave to anyone as he had need (Acts 2:45);

> Hate what is evil; cling to what is good (Rom 12:9).

It needs to be said that the language of a human rights-based approach is nothing new to various church bodies and institutions. More and more, in recent years, the language of human rights has been adopted in the work with "world service" and advocacy, as in departments in the World Council of Churches and the Lutheran World Federation. But to be able to communicate human dignity and justice, the church as the body of Christ, in its catholicity as well as its local manifestations, must deal with issues also in the depths of her identity.

OVERCOMING THE PUBLIC—PRIVATE DIVIDE

The human rights agenda is about the exercise of power and the possibilities to control and reduce misuse of power. It is far from being obvious what state actors do and what they avoid doing. The state decides rights, is supposed to implement them and controls their fulfillment. Basically, it is a system of self-regulation inside the state structure, with some possibilities for criticism from other states and the United Nations system. Put another way, it is about not allowing the authorities a monopoly in shaping justice and building a good life. A broader category of actors, voluntarily built-up organizations named non-state actors, is being taken into account more and more.

The human rights system includes a relational concept involving public and private. The church would in the human rights context be considered a private actor, in contrast to the state as the public actor. In a domestic context, on the other hand, the church will be included in the public sector, labeled civil society, while the private is the family or household. In her dissertation, focusing on corporate responsibility for human rights, Magdalena Bexell concludes that the public-private boundary is a key.[15] She found a plurality of authority relations including both public and private actors. Transnational companies more and more understand their position in the private-public sphere, taking responsibility for human rights and global governance in relation to the state as the public sphere and acting as public in relation to the workers and their families.

> The concept of governance as opposed to government opens up for the possibility of a multiplicity of authority relations, both public and private, not necessarily implying that the state loses in authority, but that its role changes.[16]

This responsibility also goes for the church as part of the public—private spectrum. But if the identity of the church includes addressed participants, its role will differ from that of, for example, business companies and international financial institutions. While companies act in their own interest and maybe on behalf of someone financially tied up to them, the church acts because it consists of addressed participants responding to the Word of God. In that way the church nullifies the distinction between public and private. The church's advantage is that its priority includes the most marginalized and stigmatized in the body of Christ.

Every time an individual is threatened by human rights violations, there is a threat to everyone, potentially facing the same destiny. At the same time, this is where we may find the most serious arguments against human rights. The women in Eastern Congo and the widow in Luke share the experience of being silenced, and not only by a strictly hierarchical

15. Bexell, *Exploring Responsibility*, 168.
16. Bexell, *Exploring Responsibility*, 190.

society. The distinction between public and private in the human rights discourse excludes some of the most serious violations against women from the concern of human rights. Violations in the domestic sphere exclude the perspectives of many women since they are considered to be abused in "private." This is slowly being corrected inside the human rights agenda but it will take more time. One important step is the recent definition of acts against the women in Congo as crimes against humanity.

If the authorities do not bother about granting the rights on the legal level, there is still an application of the human rights concept on the moral level. The Finnish researcher Pamela Slotte argues in her dissertation that human rights serve a purpose for the victim's subjective experience of a violation. Her argument is that what is identified as a violation is not in the first place an offense against norms but basically a disturbance of human relations.[17] The human rights language gives the individual a language and a safe base from where to express their reality in situations where different interpretations of a situation are incompatible. A safe haven for addressed participants is part of the identity of the body of Christ. And when there is no border between public and private, the church can continue to "nag and bother" on behalf of each individual for the sake of the chosen ones. At the same time, the church as the body of Christ is part of reconstructing disturbed relations to enable the body to continue being an inclusive relational organism.

A PEOPLE-CENTERED RESPONSIBILITY

Facing the paradox of self-regulation by the state, Abdullahi Ahmed An-Na'im, a Muslim scholar and professor of law, makes this suggestion concerning the agreed human rights:

> Since we cannot be anywhere else (than our own "home" location) long enough, with sufficient resources, understanding of the local situation, and ability to achieve sustainable change, the best we can do is to invest in empowering local actors to protect their own rights.[18]

What An-Na'im is asking for is a more "people-centered" and integrated work, done at the local level. It is a mistake to say that human rights are

17. Slotte, *Mänskliga rättigheter,* 329.
18. An-Na'im, "Towards a More," 34.

only about individuals. In the text from Luke, according to my reading, it is about the individual in the shape of a bothering widow but in an unavoidable connection with "the chosen ones" crying out day and night. It is not that the individual shall achieve her or his rights, but everyone's rights, in the same situation, excluding no-one. In opposition to Western individualism and in a discussion of human rights as "Western individual rights", African theologians and church leaders, for example Desmond Tutu, have launched the traditional concept *ubuntu*. A possible interpretation of the Zulu word ubuntu would be "I am because we are, and to the extent that we are, I am."[19] To my understanding, that agrees with the intention of universal human rights. The Universal Declaration of Human Rights states in *Article 1*: "All human beings are born free and equal in dignity and rights." The point is that rights are for each and every single person, since human beings exist in relationship with one another.

Once again, back for a moment to the text from Luke. In modern human rights-language taken from the human rights-based approach, the widow would be named a "rights-holder" and the judge a "duty-bearer." Thus the parable can be considered to be about demanding the rights from duty-bearers and thereby changing life for people who are rights-holders. In a human rights-based approach there is a need for participation by the rights-holder, demanding the rights from a position of vulnerability, and challenging the responsibility and duties of the duty-bearer standing in a position of power.[20]

The perspective of rights-holders is maybe not always easy for church-structures to adopt and especially not when the history of the church involves being part of the state structure. There is a long history in the church of perspectives *talking* about compassion, mercy, care-giving and even charity, with an imperative taken from the Good Samaritan. In a way this also goes for giving aid and assistance on the development level, though it is not possible to generalize. The concept of rights-holders aims to reject the idea that persons not being granted their rights are victims. As created in the image of God, dignity and justice are their rights. It also shifts the perspective away from the state and onto the people as actors.

A "people-centered" approach indicates participation based on a broad popular partaking, including male and female. The church as the

19. Jacques, *Resisting the Intolerable*, 42.
20. Theis, *Right-based Monitoring*.

body of Christ does have the possibility of creating an identity and utilizing instruments, thus becoming a vehicle for people-centered rights-holder's involvement and allowing each individual to be part of the solution, on different levels in society.

This way of changing power and control is enabling a change in human relations and the life of the individual. The rights-holder may need a forum for "bothering the authorities" and, if necessary, be supported by others crying out day and night. Whatever happens, they need a people-centred structure that helps them not to give up, and a structure that they can trust will include "addressed participants" who continue struggling even if they as rights-holders will loose their life in the struggle against the perpetrators. It is a process of liberating God's people to be addressed participants.

A PEOPLE-CENTERED DISTRIBUTIVE JUSTICE

What is the future of the women sitting outside the hospital in Eastern Congo? I would not be surprised if—assuming that they conceive of the concept of human rights—they would consider it impossible for them to benefit from human rights. Neither would I be surprised if they regard the church as an institution playing with their perpetrators. Yet, they continue to pray, they do not give up and they continue to remember their baptism into Christ and the celebration of the Eucharist, believing they are still part of the true body of Christ without any borders in space and time.

Still they are bound to a spot of soil, with their physical and psychological problems under terrible circumstances, without any possibility of comparing with, for example, an average Swedish member of the same body of Christ. Human rights violations can be painful wherever they occur but there is also the question of resources and the way present-day states want to preserve their privileges and unjust levels of development. To find out, all you need is some figures concerning the Democratic Republic of Congo, compared with Sweden and the United States. The following table of economic performance gives an idea of the enormous gap:[21]

---

21. *Human Development Report*, 280.

	GDP per capita US$ 2005	Annual growth rate (%) 1990–2005	Human development rank
United States	41 890	2.1	12
Sweden	39 637	2.1	6
DR of Congo	123	-5.2	168

The Democratic Republic of Congo is ranked 168 out of 177 countries. The difference with the United States and Sweden in terms of GDP per capita is huge. The level of USD 123 in DR Congo shows that women there are living in one of the poorest countries in the world. Women from villages in the remote eastern part of the vast country, stigmatized and excluded from family and society, have virtually no financial resources.

Even if the women can achieve their basic human rights, there is still the question of power and control on the global level. In the arena of public—private, new global actors are stepping in, for example multinational companies. The nation-state will loose influence while other interests gain control. The South-African theologian H. Russel Botman has warned about the future of the human rights discourse in the African context:

> The human rights discourse in itself will for the foreseeable future continue to suffer from the human and political consequences of economic globalization.[22]

From the Asian context, Vandana Shiva has repeatedly warned that human rights have not been globalized while human wrongs have been turned into law. She is talking about trade agreements and WTO rules, which she labels "genocide." Medical patents are keeping the price hundreds of times higher than if India had been allowed to produced the drug. Another concern is genetically modified seed, which is forcing farmers to incur huge debts.[23] One more example is taken from the *Human Development Report*.

> Climate change is now a scientifically established fact. The exact impact of greenhouse gas emission is not easy to forecast and there

---

22. Botman, "Human Dignity," 29.
23. Shiva, *Skydda eller skövla?* and Shiva, "Mänsklig orätt."

FOR THE SAKE OF THE WORLD

is a lot of uncertainty in the science when it comes to predictive capability.[24]

People in Peru account for 0.1 percent of the world's carbon emissions but will pay a high price for the glacial melting caused by emissions in other countries. Estimates indicate that in sub-Saharan Africa an additional 75 million to 250 million people could have their livelihoods "compromised by a combination of drought, rising temperature and increased water stress." Vietnam, Bangladesh, the Maldives, several Pacific islands and islands in the Caribbean are vulnerable in this new situation.[25] These are just examples and of course beyond the control of people on the local level even if they achieve their basic human rights.

It is about power structures and it is about control. If one, apparently successful, part of the Body of Christ is living with a per capita GDP around USD 40,000 and another part of the Body with around USD 100, then there is a problem of justice. In the discussion that followed the South African Truth and Reconciliation Commission, theologians have talked about the need of distributive justice, biblically referring to the notion of the jubilee in Leviticus.[26] Russel Botman asks for a redistribution of wealth that goes beyond the ordinary social security responsibilities of the state.[27] It could be claimed that persons recovering from severe human rights violations need not only justice in relation to the violation/crime but also a part of a distributive justice.

Will there always be women causing the chosen ones to cry out day and night? God will see that they get justice and do so quickly, as stated by Luke, but it may take some bothering. The Body of Christ in its identity includes, in its local manifestations as well as in the Body over space and time, the addressed participants ready to be troublesome, ready to work for passionate change.

WHAT ABOUT THE "JUDGE"?

In the text from Luke, the judge finally changed his mind and granted the rights-holder her right. But what about the perpetrators and human rights

24. *Human Development Report*, V.
25. *Human Development Report*, 114–16.
26. Tsele, "Kairos and Jubilee."
27. Botman, "Human Dignity," 31.

abusers—the duty-bearers—that are not granting rights or even violating rights? The international human rights system has set up criminal courts and tribunals dealing with the serious perpetrators. Punishment for the abuser and justice and retribution for the victim are needed and maybe the process includes both forgiveness and reconciliation. In the footsteps of the South African Truth and Reconciliation Commission, several similar commissions have been set up to deal with injustices and reconciliation. There is also a group that is often forgotten in these processes: people looking on, bystanders without the possibility to interfere but forced to witness what is going on, or people just not taking action. The church as a people- and rights-holders-oriented body with an identity as addressed participants has a major contribution to make in this situation, with instruments handed down through the incarnation for achieving forgiveness, reconciliation and love. Justice will enable peace and provide space for reconciliation and forgiveness.

Mirsolav Volf deals, in *The End of Memory*, with what happens to the memory of wrongs suffered. He remarks that if we remember wrongs suffered, we defer to the wishes of the evil-doers and also pay too much respect to evil itself.

> We will not "forget" so as to be able to rejoice; we will rejoice and *therefore* let those memories slip out of our minds! The reason for our non-remembrance of wrongs will be the same as its cause: Our minds will be rapt in the goodness of God and in the goodness of God's new world, and the memories of wrongs will wither away like plants without water.[28]

REMEMBER—SHE IS BOTHERING ME

If experience—in one way or another—plays a role, the identity of the church is not given once and for all. New situations will always challenge traditions, just as new understandings of the relation to the incarnation and to love in Jesus Christ open up for new responses to how to be a Christian today. At the same time, that openness is seen as being faithful to the Scripture and to tradition.

In common with the human rights discourse, the church as addressed participants sees human dignity, justice, and aspirations for a

---

28. Volf, *The End of Memory*, 214.

good existence as indispensable aspects of human life. Thus, there seems to be a reciprocal interest and unity in task between the church and the human rights discourse in dealing with violations, sufferings and oppression in the world. The human rights system has developed ideas and instruments that may be useful in strengthening the identity of the church. And a church with these issues at heart may challenge a dynamic human rights-discourse in key issues. That seems to be a way of reading both the needs of people today and the biblical story.

The church as addressed participants has to be people-centered, creating an identity through the inclusion of the suffering parts of the body of Christ, comprising everyone as an image of God. With a focus on marginalized and stigmatized people, this is an unavoidable item in the totality of characteristics in the identity of the church. By adopting a people-oriented rights-holders approach to analyzing and emphasizing violations against human beings, the church will be a people-centered actor, reducing the distinction in the human rights discourse between public and private.

It is important that the body of Christ, the church, manages to recover the claim for justice. The church has to be instrumental for the cry coming day and night from one individual in need of rights, since if one is suffering—all are suffering. The church-organism cannot be satisfied until its own people as one body willingly cry out. The human rights violations are not the final word in God's intentions.

Conclusions from the relationship between human rights and the church would not only enable church members to successfully relate to those outside their own group but also be theologically fruitful, promote values, and give church members as addressed participants a sense of corporate identity and mission. A troublesome church, consisting of addressed participants that keep on bothering and wearing out the powers and authorities of the world, may be a perspective with new impulses to the concept "folk" in folk-church.

BIBLIOGRAPHY

Ackermann, Denise. "Tamar's Cry: Re-Reading an Ancient Text in the Midst of an HIV and AIDS Pandemic." In *Grant Me Justice: HIV/AIDS & Gender Readings of the Bible*, edited by Musa W. Dube, and Musimbi R.A. Kanyoro, 27–59. Maryknoll, N.Y.: Orbis, 2004.

Amjad-Ali, Charles. *Passion for Change. Reflections on the Healing Miracles in St. Mark*. Rawalpindi: Christian Study Centre, 1989.

An-Na'im, Abdullahi Ahmed. "Towards a More People-Centered Human Rights Movement." In *Mänskliga rättigheter—från forskningens frontlinjer. Human Rights— from the Frontiers of research*, edited by Diana Amnéus and Göran Gunner, Uppsala: Iustus förlag, 2003.

Bailey, Kenneth E. *Poet & Peasant. A Literary-Cultural Approach to the Parables in Luke*. Grand Rapids: Eerdmans, 1976.

Bexell, Magdalena. *Exploring Responsibility. Public and Private in Human Rights Protection*. Lund: Department of Political Science, Lund University, 2005.

Botman, H. Russel. "Human Dignity and Economic Globalization." In *Building a Human Rights Culture. South African and Swedish Perspectives*, edited by Karin Sporre and H. Russel Botman. Falun: Högskolan Dalarna, 2003.

Brandon Scott, Bernard. *Hear Then the Parable. A Commentary on the Parables of Jesus*. Minneapolis: Fortress, 1989.

Cavanaugh, William T. *Torture and Eucharist*. Oxford: Blackwell Publishing, 1998.

Fernandez, Eleazar S. *Reimagining the Human. Theological Anthropology in response to Systematic Evil*. St. Louis, Missouri: Chalic, 2004.

Fitzmyer, Joseph A. *The Gospel According to Luke (X–XXIV)*. Garden City, New York: Doubleday, 1985.

Hochschild, Adam. *King Leopold's Ghost: A story of greed, terror, and heroism in Colonial Africa*. Boston: Houghton Mifflin, 1998.

Human Development Report 2007/2008. New York: United Nations Development Programme, 2007, 292. Online: http://hdr.undp.org/en/media/HDR_20072008_EN_Complete.pdf.

Jacques, Geneviève. *Resisting the Intolerable. Guided by a Human Rights Compass*. Geneva: WCC Publications, 2007.

Newlands, George. *Christ and Human Rights*. Hampshire: Ashgate, 2006.

Shiva, Vandana. *Skydda eller skövla?: patent, etik och nykolonialism*. Stockholm: Ordfront, 2003.

———. "Mänsklig orätt har upphöjts till lag." In *Mänskliga rättigheter och samhällets skyldigheter: en antologi från MR-dagarna 2004*, edited by Göran Gunner, and Anders Mellbourn. Stockholm: Ordfront, 2005.

Slotte, Pamela. *Mänskliga rättigheter, moral och religion. Om de mänskliga rättigheterna som moraliskt och juridiskt begrepp i en pluralistisk värld*. Åbo: Åbo Akademis Förlag, 2005.

Theis, Joachim. *Rights-based Monitoring and Evaluation. A Discussion Paper*. Save the Children, April 2003.

Tsele, Molefe. "Kairos and Jubilee." In *To Rememberand to Heal: Theological and Psychological Reflections on Truth and Reconciliation*, editied by H. Russel Botman, and Robin M. Petersen. Cape Town: Human and Rousseau, 1996.

Villa-Vincencio, Charles. "Theology and Human Rights." In *Human Rights & Religion. A Reader*, edited by Liam Gearson. Brighton: Sussex Academic, 2002.

Volf, Miroslav. *The End of Memory. Remembering Rightly in a Violent World*. Grand Rapids: Eerdmans, 2006.

"People of Faith"—a Different Kind of Body Economy?

ANTJE JACKELÉN

THE CONTEXT: A VIEW FROM OUTSIDE

Some time in the late summer of 2008 I received an e-mail that was quite different from most other messages that show up in my inbox. I quote the mail at length, because it makes some relevant points about the ecclesiological context of Western Europe:

> This autumn former prime minister Tony Blair will be joining Yale University as a Howland Distinguished Fellow. In partnership with Yale Divinity School professor Miroslav Volf, he will be teaching a course called "Faith and Globalization" to students from the Divinity School, the School of Management, the Graduate School of Arts and Sciences, and Yale College. Students will examine the ways in which religious faiths influence political decisions, economic development, and business operations in various cultures around the world.... The fourth week of the course will focus on "Secularization, Religious Resurgence, and Multiple Modernities." The session will look at the theory of secularization and challenges to that theory. Students will examine sociological studies of the global "resurgence" of religion and will reflect on the reasons why secularization has failed to take root across the world.... Special attention will be given to Western Europe as an apparently anomalous case in need of explanation. The session will conclude by considering the implications o the apparent permanence of religion as a vital cultural factor.... For session four we would like to focus on Sweden...

"People of Faith"—a Different Kind of Body Economy?

This e-mail from Yale University sets the scene quite nicely for my attempt to offer a phenomenological and somewhat kaleidoscopic perspective on ecclesiological issues. I note several points of interest here.

- A former prime minister devotes part of his retirement to teach a course about faith and globalization.
- The course in question is deliberately transdisciplinary, involving students of Yale Divinity School as well as the School of Management and arts and sciences. The topic "religion" transgresses traditional patterns of compartmentalization.
- It is presupposed that religion—in the shape of religious faiths—influences political decisions, economic development and global business.
- It is also presupposed that modernity is so diverse that it is justified to speak of multiple modernities.
- It is further presupposed that the theory of secularization is and has to be questioned because secularization has not occurred as predicted and we in fact see a resurgence of religion.
- And finally: Western Europe is an anomaly—and therefore a case in need of explanation.

I agree with the course planners at Yale that Sweden qualifies particularly well as an example of the Western European anomaly. In fact, Sweden is exceptional in at least two respects. On the one hand, Sweden is according to relevant statistics undisputedly one of the most secularized countries in the world and thus seems predisposed to resist the resurgence of religion; on the other hand, 74% of the population are members of one specific church, Church of Sweden,[1] which seems to suggest that Sweden is not even in need of any resurgence of religion! This looks like a strange reality that rightly puzzles people who look at Sweden from abroad.

The religious situation is certainly not as clear as it looked to a Washington Post writer who in connection with the funeral of John Paul II in 2005 spoke of the Vatican as "109 acres of faith in a European Sea of

---

1. Until 2000, Church of Sweden (Lutheran) was a state church, which largely explains the high level of membership. After the disestablishment of Church of Sweden, membership has dropped each year, but at a slower rate in the past three years.

unbelief."[2] Secularized Sweden may present itself as a perfect part of that European Sea of unbelief. However, if you care to taste the water of that sea, you can't miss that it carries pretty much of the distinctly salty flavor of the Christian gospel.

Swedish welfare systems reveal traits of secularized Christianity, especially in the shape of the Lutheran tradition. Although far from being the only valid explanation, there is some truth to the statement that the welfare system of the secular state is a proof of the success of the social and ethical teachings of the church.

Let me borrow the voice of a journalist and TV news anchor of quite some reputation to illustrate the complicated dynamics of secular and religious in Swedish society:

> When it comes to questions of life and death, personal relationships and spirituality, politics has no answers—when it comes to health, happiness and community, power has no tools. Love, warmth and care cannot be achieved by election promises or packages of measures to be taken. . . . Adding a non-material dimension to descriptions of reality has been complicated in the Swedish context.

Yet, he concludes after referring to some contemporary challenges:

> [T]his certainly is an eye-opener for those who think that spirituality and belief in God are irrelevant.[3]

Sociological surveys leave no doubt that according to standard parameters, Sweden is a success story of secularization. Nevertheless, even Sweden has not been untouched by the "resurgence" of religion. In recent years, the number of newspaper articles, columns, blogs, radio and TV programs discussing religion has increased at a remarkable rate. A rather generalizing impression from browsing these sources over a period of time suggests that they convey mostly three types of view: a deliberately positive assessment of religion; a rigorous and at times aggressive campaigning against religion; or constructive contributions dealing with the widespread lack of knowledge about religion and seeking deeper understanding of religious traditions.

---

2. Will, "Suicide."
3. Adaktusson, "Det mest försummade."

"People of Faith"—a Different Kind of Body Economy?

A Swedish journalist notes that Danish futurologists have reported that between 1995 and 2004 the number of newspaper articles including the word "God" increased by 234 per cent. For texts including the phrase "belief in God" the increase was as much as 3033 per cent, which leads him to the conclusion: "Modernity has not led to atheism, but rather to a luxuriant private religiosity where everybody is their own bishop."[4]

From this, one may conclude that post-secularization is a reality even in Sweden. With the "resurgence" of religion we see two apparently opposite trends operating simultaneously, namely the return of God on the one hand and the rise of an aggressive atheism on the other. These two are both part of a dynamics unfolding in a climate that regards religiosity primarily as a question of individual choice and practice.

This perspective, mainly informed by observations from "outside," needs to be complemented by a perspective that takes a closer look at the inner dynamics of spiritual identity in Sweden and connects to significant theological and philosophical developments.

THE CONTEXT: A VIEW FROM INSIDE

Swedish writer Torgny Lindgren's novel *Norrlands Akvavit* articulates the tension between faith and modernity in remarkable ways. As always, multiple interpretations are possible. One may say that *Norrlands Akvavit* is about the transition from Christian revival to a modernity that has no need whatsoever of God, faith or religion. This would mark ecclesiological thought as superfluous and meaningless. One may also say, however, that the book describes a transition from doubt to a faith that includes the very opposite of faith: maybe it is only as a renegade that one is able to find a way home. This in turn would make the theological study of spiritual development and praxis a priority. In other words, what we see, may be an ecclesiologically frustrating, yet theologically exciting scenario!

Norrlands Akvavit is the story of the revivalist Olof Helmersson who after five decades returns to the Northern Swedish villages he once won for Christ. This time he comes in order to de-Christianize them, because he has become convinced that there is no God, no heaven and no hell. Things do not quite go his way, however. In some ways, people in the region have already de-Christianized themselves. The saleswoman in the liquor store says about her coiffure: "When I was very young I belonged

---

4. Söderberg, "Privatiserad Gud."

to a congregation where we all had such topknots. Everybody was saved. I got rid of salvation pretty fast. But kept the hairdo."[5] When Helmersson's bus had passed the place from where one used to have a good view of the chapel, he remarks to the driver: "That's strange. I couldn't see the chapel." "It burnt down," the driver said. "And nobody cared about rebuilding it."[6]

The longer Helmersson travels around the villages, the stronger the paradox becomes. "What he had thought or said deep inside himself, he declared, was nobody's concern, . . . it was an affair between himself and the God who does not exist."[7] One of those converted by Helmersson fifty years earlier explains: "I don't believe. But I lack doubt. . . . Now we believe what we want. And on our own. That is part of our greatness."[8] In the end Lindgren has Helmersson deliver a brilliant summary of his mission: "There is no eternity, he said. That's why I've come back. I must put things right. And recant. Everything. Before we all enter eternity."[9]

What is the message here? That it is only as apostates that we can find our way home? The paradoxes in *Norrlands Akvavit* recall the tension that is so central to Lutheran theology—that of *simul iustus et peccator*: justified and sinner all at once, home-comer and renegade at the same time. In exposing this paradox as inherent in much of the spirituality that has shaped Sweden, Lindgren gives a thought-provoking background to the dynamics in the Swedish context as it can be observed from 'outside'.

For a theologian, it is rewarding to read the novel also as a comment on the development of theology over the past fifty years. The 1960s saw the culmination of the so-called God-is-dead theologies. In their wake, new God-language was born. Here are some examples: "God is more than necessary" (the German theologian Eberhard Jüngel),[10] "God without being" (the French theologian Jean-Luc Marion)[11] and "God the event" (the American philosopher John Caputo).[12] This language moves God-talk to

---

5. Lindgren, *Norrlands Akvavit*, 8.
6. Lindgren, *Norrlands Akvavit*, 12.
7. Lindgren, *Norrlands Akvavit*, 97.
8. Lindgren, *Norrlands Akvavit*, 126.
9. Lindgren, *Norrlands Akvavit*, 140.
10. Jüngel, *Gott als Geheimnis*, 30.
11. Marion, *God Without Being*.
12. Caputo, *Weakness*.

a ground that lies beyond the realm of abstract theism, because theism as abstract idea is always concerned with the necessity of God. A "more than necessary God" is a category that theism cannot deal with. It is only in the sphere of a God who is more than necessary that it makes sense to say, as Lindgren does of Helmersson, that something is "an affair between himself and the God who does not exist." Without an opening beyond the God of abstract theism, such a statement is merely absurd.

In more abstract terms, I would say that this leads to the conclusion that we are in need of a more rigorous enlightenment and a softer ontology. We need an enlightenment that is enlightened about the risks of freezing into dogma what is the story and experience of an event; and we need a more open philosophy and theology that take seriously the fact and the experience that we are always exposed to uncertainty. We are exposed to the undecidability that marks the core of being—an insight that must be credited to the achievements of quantum physics—and to the contextuality that requires perpetual translation between texts and contexts under the spell and the promise of the ambiguity of language—an insight to be counted as the great achievement of hermeneutics.

This in turn has consequences for atheism. In the words of Italian philosopher Gianni Vattimo: "The end of metaphysics and the death of the moral God have liquidated the philosophical basis of atheism."[13] Put in positive terms, this means: a softer ontology and the move beyond the necessary God have deprived atheism of its philosophical basis. Vattimo observes that with the fall of modern theism, even atheism became an impossible position, because it is the negation of theism. If God is more than necessary, there is no point in the atheistic critique that wants to get rid of the idea of God by showing that it is a non-necessary idea. If the foremost statement about God is no longer that God exists, then also the negation of God's existence becomes a rather pointless exercise. The atheism that is a mirror image of theism has lost a lot of its base. This is quite obvious as long as atheism relies on arguments that reflect a rather positivist epistemology, that rely on a dualistic worldview where natural and supernatural as well as immanent and transcendent are each other's opposites, and that are trapped in the idea of an exclusively abstract, authoritarian,

---

13. Quoted in Robbins, "Introduction," 17. (Originally in: Gianni Vattimo. After Christianity, trans. Luca d'Isanto. New York: Columbia University Press, 2002. 17).

transcendent God. In a time when dualisms have been relativized—or better: relationalized—atheism will need new theoretic foundations.

This, of course, does not mean that the discourse of late modernity can prove God more than any other discourse. One can say, however, that an atheism that is stuck with a second coming of European Enlightenment philosophy will not achieve much. It misses out on newer developments in philosophy, theology and anthropology. Moreover, by uncritically presupposing that a European thought tradition automatically and unchangeably owns global validity, it does not meet the needs of a post-colonial and globalized world very well. What is most alarming, though, is the well-grounded suspicion that it will fail to build up the spiritual capacity needed to meet the great challenges facing all humanity. The atheism I am speaking of here, routinely defines faith as an inferior way of knowing, and not much else. This is a rather limited view: it falls short of seeing that in many faith traditions, faith is understood to be primarily about relationships of trust and confidence and about hope.

In light of these developments, it becomes possible to revaluate even Friedrich Nietzsche's atheism. It is no longer necessary to interpret Nietzsche's critique of religion as the negation of all values and hence as a straight road to nihilism. Rather, his passionate critique can be interpreted as an attempt to set truth and values free from their seemingly supra-historic and transcendent captivity.

German philosopher Jürgen Habermas provides us with some clues that point in the same direction. Reason that takes seriously its own critique and its own limits cannot help but transcend itself toward something other and different, he claims. This kind of transcendence happens without any previous or explicit theological intention.[14] Therefore, Habermas concludes in his well-known conversation with then Cardinal Ratzinger: it is in the interest of both philosophy and democracy to handle those cultural sources that feed the norm consciousness of citizens with great care, and to facilitate open and complementary processes of learning.[15]

These literary, theological and philosophical perspectives on the ecclesiological context suggest that the dynamics of secularization and

---

14. "Ohne anfänglich theologische Absicht überschreitet sich auf diesen Wegen eine ihre Grenzen inne werdende Vernunft auf ein Anderes hin . . ." Habermas and Ratzinger, *Dialektik*, 29.

15. Habermas and Ratzinger, *Dialektik*, 32f.

"People of Faith"—a Different Kind of Body Economy?

resurgence of religion is present also in Sweden. How do ecclesiology and the ecclesial reality correspond to this context?

ECCLESIOLOGY AND THE CHURCH AS A SOCIAL BODY

Talking about the church as a social body focuses on two things: social relationships within the body and the relationship between the church as body of Christ and society. Both are dependent on the self-understanding of a church and its way of articulating its vision and mission. Let us turn to a concrete example:

In Church of Sweden, a vision statement has been circulated that was originally formulated by the information and communication department at the Church's national level; it has since been adopted also at other levels in the church. The statement says: "Church of Sweden shall be a church to which people have a positive relationship and which people feel happy to be part of."

When interviewed about their feelings about this vision statement, church workers and active laypeople tend to commend the positive tone and express a fairly high level of contentment with the way it is formulated. At that point in the conversation, I often ask people to replace 'Church of Sweden' with the name of any association of their choice and liking. It is only then that people begin to be confounded and to wonder whether having a vision that would fit a whole range of different organizations is good enough. It is also quite clear that the vision statement in question is oriented toward a consumer model. Its accomplishment can be checked by a survey that polls consumer satisfaction.

In contrast, one may wish to look at an alternative vision statement, such as that of the Evangelical Lutheran Church in America (ELCA). It runs like this: "Marked with the cross of Christ forever, we are claimed, gathered and sent for the sake of the world." Here, consumer satisfaction will not do as a criterion of successful implementation. In this case, one would have to look for differences made in the world by people identifying as members of the body of those "marked with the cross of Christ forever," that is, the baptized.

Consumer-satisfaction models of the church tend to center on the church as an organization and to regard its members as consumers of a range of services offered. Consequently, the church gets identified with its employed staff and its elected councils. Critics point to a risky equation that eventually will undermine the very existence of the church. It goes like this: faith perceived of as a private matter only + the church looked upon mainly as an institution + leadership exercised by professionals only + members regarded as clients = a paralyzed church.

In contrast, make-a-difference models of the church have a tendency to focus on sending rather than service, on activity rather than consumption. Members are 'sellers' rather than clients, as it were. In this paradigm, faith would not be a private matter only. It would be mostly personal and as such would have public implications. The relative stability of the church as an institution would be regarded as an asset, yet emphasis would be on organic and changing relationships. Leadership would ideally be exercised by combining the expertise of professionals with all Christians' baptismal vocation—in Lutheran tradition famously called the priesthood of all believers.

When asked about the rationale behind their ecclesiological model, leaders of the ELCA describe a process that is shifting the focus from an understanding of congregations as communities of care to an understanding of congregations and parishioners as missionaries of grace.[16] Internal church work aims at building both community and capacity by training and exercising leadership. Leadership is seen as teamwork, shared by clergy and laypeople. The aim is to help congregations to develop a sense of purpose—to be able to identify what God is calling them to do. Where emphasis is more on sending than on receiving people into a community of care, the public and political expression of faith will be in the center of recognition.

The following excerpt from a column by Martin E. Marty is a case in point. He describes a worship service on Super Bowl Sunday 1986 at the Apostolic Church of God, a community church in Woodlawn, Chicago:

> At that service, 18 people were baptized, we honored a couple hundred members who had visited prisoners in the week past and, of course, we gloried in the music. . . . Churches like the Apostolic Church of God, Trinity United Church of Christ and other largely black congregations are the soul of this city. High school kids sing in their choirs. Hundreds of sick and homebound are visited by their parishioners. These churches don't preach politics, but they

---

16. Personal communication with the author at the Headquarters of the ELCA in Chicago, April 2008.

cannot but be political, because the *polis*, the city, is the arena for the works of God as they interpret and experience them.[17]

The comparison between ecclesial visions in Church of Sweden and American churches sheds light on how historical contexts influence the ways in which churches envision their status and their tasks. Differences in church-state relationships notwithstanding, there are common developments. Contemporary ecclesial reasoning often takes its point of departure from a scenario where the church was located at the center of society. Under those circumstances, the church played a major role in training respectable citizens and equipping them morally. Moreover, there was a relationship of mutual blessing between church and culture: church blesses culture and culture blesses church, as was the idea in German Kulturprotestantismus. This phase was followed by a process of more or less intense secularization. The church moved and was moved to the fringe. Its contribution to citizenship training diminished. The relationship between church and culture diversified. Partnership still exists, but only in combination with a rather active distancing and critiquing on both sides. Instead of representing the standard model of a good citizen, the self-identified active practitioner of Christian faith now tends to be the exception from the rule of normalcy. This phase in turn is now being followed by processes of adaptation to a multicultural and multireligious environment. In many places, religion has gained new importance as an ethnic and cultural marker. While this may have both positive and negative consequences, it certainly does bring something new to the self-understanding of churches that had learned to think of themselves as institutions that once were at the center and then became used to dwelling on the fringes.

The multicultural and multireligious environment is of course not new everywhere. It has been the state of the art in numerous places around the world. But it is only now, in the age of postcolonial and postmodern critique, that it has more seriously entered the minds of those who still produce the theological thinking that predominates. In our days, multicultural and multireligious interfaces give rise to new kinds of experiences that present a challenge to most traditional ecclesiological models.

Ecclesiology usually starts from the presupposition that there is a definable entity that can be called church and then moves on to describ-

17. Marty, "Among royalty," 39.

ing the marks that identify the church distinctly as the body of Christ. Even though marks and models of the church may be presented in a descriptive manner, they clearly have a normative purpose of shaping the body of Christ in a certain way.

However new they are, multireligious experiences add something to established concepts of the body of Christ; they may even change the experience of the body in such a way that a new body economy emerges.

This is how I think it works: Where multireligious experiences are sought and made, overlapping consensus and overlapping loyalty are being formed. This is not the same as the phenomenon that goes by the name of syncretism. Rather, I am talking about those common experiences that build on the encounter between people who are deeply and consciously rooted in their own tradition, yet willing to share and learn from others. Such encounters are taking place, for example, between Muslims, Jews and Christians in the shape of interfaith banquets, iftar meals and interfaith worship services. Events of mutual hospitality create a consciousness about new possibilities of consensus. For example, Muslims, Jews and Christians can come to realize that in sharing hospitality with each other, they share in that moment, in spite of their differences in the teachings and the practices of their religion, a stronger experience of mutual understanding or even communion with each other than each of them does with other parts of their own faith tradition.

This is an example of what I call overlapping consensus. The basic difference in identity is preserved, yet areas of potentially powerful and empowering consensus emerge and are experienced. This does not compromise the 'old' identity, but adds a new one that actually can both strengthen and expand the old one. Where people identify as "people of faith" in addition to being for example Buddhists, Jews, Muslims or Christians, a new body economy is established and experienced. Body awareness is changed by experienced hospitality.

Over time, such experiences will change perspectives and attitudes toward consensus or lack thereof within the Christian family. It is likely that these processes will be accelerated where overlapping consensus expresses itself in common diapraxis, that is, in socially relevant practices engaging a common problem.

In other words, a changed body economy, in which people of different religions co-identify as people of faith, has consequences that are both ecclesiological and political. A quote from UN Secretary General Ban Ki-moon will illustrate this. It is from a speech in which he calls on people of faith to support the struggle against global warming:

> . . . Slowing, indeed reversing, these trends have emerged as the defining challenge of our age. It requires both your prayers and your participation. Indeed, success in the fight against climate change is hard to contemplate without the input and energy of *men and women of faith*.
>
> All of you can help inspire millions of people around the world to become better stewards of our planet. You can guide them towards healthier, more sustainable lifestyles. . . . And you can reinforce the belief, fundamental to all religions, that we have a sacred obligation to leave the world a better place for those who will follow.[18]

CONSEQUENCES FOR TRADITIONAL ECCLESIOLOGIES? FROM PURITY TO HYBRIDITY

One fruitful way of studying ecclesiology over time is to look at different, often co-existing, models of the church and analyze their characteristic traits, their strengths and weaknesses in relation to each other, their respective contexts and the bulk of Christian theology.[19] As Avery Dulles remarks in his classical "Models of the Church," the dominant model in connection with Vatican II was "people of God."

In our days, it is worth exploring what the "people of faith" model that is knocking at our doors with some persistence can contribute to a Christian ecclesiology for our time. Are we witnessing a paradigm-shift, when it comes to describing the nature and norms of faith communities? Or is the "people-of-faith" model merely a blind alley? Or an elitist concept viable for fringe groups of intellectuals? Can the people-of-faith model be combined with a consumer model or only with a make-a-difference model of the church? These and other relevant questions are worth deeper exploration than this essay can provide. However, some preliminary thoughts regarding possible consequences for traditional ecclesiologies will be offered here.

---

18. http://www.un.org/News/Press/docs//2007/sgsm11276.doc.htm (my emphasis).
19. Cf. Dulles, *Models*, and Kärkkäinen, *Ecclesiology*.

The people-of-faith model will have repercussions on traditional distinctions of what can count as adiaphora and what is or comes close to the level of a status confessionis. For instance, from a people-of-faith perspective it will be even harder to attribute much relevance to the distinction suggested in *Dominus Iesus* between what can count as a church and what should be regarded only as church-like associations.[20]

In general, a people-of-faith approach will favor normative practices over against conceptual distinctions. It will value "walking together" over "thinking the same thoughts." The normative practices will draw on two main motifs that can be found in major religious traditions, namely hospitality as a holy duty and seeking the welfare of society. In the Christian tradition, these are reflected in Hebrews 13:2: "Do not neglect to show hospitality to strangers, for by doing that some have entertained angels without knowing it," and Jeremiah 29:7: "Seek the welfare of the city where I have sent you into exile, and pray to the Lord on its behalf, for in its welfare you will find your welfare."

As indicated, these motifs can create strong overlapping consensus while allowing for differences in the rationale behind common praxis. They serve the purpose of creating beneficial praxis for a given context. They do not have the goal of creating united institutions. Thus, they have a different focus than much of Christian ecumenism: in light of the imperative of hospitality, they would question practices of baptized Christians denying each other Eucharistic hospitality; in light of seeking the welfare "of the city," they would question visible union within the institutionalized Church as a prioritized goal.

To put the question bluntly, what is "wrong" with the ecclesiologies that are implied by Christian ecumenism? In short, they are mainly driven by an ideal of purity, whereas the new context is increasingly driven by hybridity.

What does that mean? When it comes to philosophy and theology, it is our growing familiarity with contemporary voices, nourished in other cultural and philosophical contexts than those of the West, that has opened our eyes to see syncretistic developments also in the heart and history of Western philosophy and theology. In theology, Asian, African and Latin American voices have raised the awareness that a *theologia absoluta et pura*, an absolute and pure theology, has never existed and cannot be

---

20. Congregation for the Doctrine of the Faith, *Dominus Iesus*.

the norm for doing theology. Rather, the norm must be a theology that can motivate and nourish hope. This does not happen by means of an absolute theology, but rather by means of a re-solute theology—a theology resolved to pursue the critical and self-critical reflection on the contents and effects of religious traditions. Such a theology will not worship purity as a value in itself, it will be prepared to get dirty in its earthy business.

A crucial choice has to be made about how one wants to view what is other—be it another faith tradition or, as often the case in Sweden, secularization. The basic alternative is to view the other as a positive or a negative other. Secularization can certainly present itself as the foe of Christian faith. But we must not forget that secularization also is a partner and even a fruit of Christianity. Therefore, we should relate to it not as a negative other, but as a positive other.[21]

If the other is perceived as a negative other, arguments from context always carry the suspicion of being merely arguments from convenience—giving in to a hostile world and hence betraying "classical faith," however one chooses to define such a problematic term. Arguments from convenience are likely to be second rate, especially for religious communities that take the content of their own faith traditions seriously.

However, if we accept the hypothesis that attention to context by default equals an argument from convenience (because the context is a priori defined as en encounter with a negative other), I am afraid we are putting ourselves on a slippery slope, because then an argument from convenience means surrendering to the circumstances (or euphemized as: change for practical purposes), which is taken to be the same as selling out the treasures of tradition. This line of reasoning would determine the outcome right from the start; we would most certainly end up with a conflict scenario that puts a society pushing away from Christian values in opposition to a pressed church on the retreat, defending apodictically defined moral codes.

Instead, I would like to suggest a more complex understanding of the notion of context.

I find the issue of contextualization too precious and too important for the future of theology, churches and church communion to have it drowned in an ocean of convenience. In fact, I am convinced that to be truly contextual is not especially convenient. Or maybe, by analogy with

---

21. Cf. Jackelén, "What is 'Secular'?"

the notion of cheap and costly grace, we should say that there is both cheap and costly contextualization. Cheap contextualization would lead to mindless adaptation or antagonism of church and state/society. From a Christian perspective, the ensuing dynamics would all too often look like fighting a losing battle. Costly contextualization is different. It has the potential of bringing about serious dialogue and change in all actors involved. It would bind together people and powers of good will in a relationship of critical solidarity. This contextualization could be imagined along Lindgrenian and Lutheran lines: only as apostates can we find the way home, and it is in the messy existence as *simul iustus et peccator* that the gospel can be lived by humans. This makes for a different dynamics—a difference that is by no means trivial.

The public dimension of Christian teaching and practice cannot be abandoned. However, its expression, especially in secular and multicultural societies, must change in order to stay even remotely close to whatever we mean by "the tradition." Again, this view creates a dynamic that is different from one built on convenience or competition as the only alternatives.

Conversations in churches and between churches should not start from a general understanding of the other as a negative other, in regard to whom the church needs to mark difference and distance. I see two potentially harmful implications of such an approach: firstly, it encourages the creation of a self-image that is defined by what one is against rather than what one is for, and secondly, it encourages the misunderstanding that society is constantly changing and moving towards a legislative climate that is increasingly hostile to traditional Christian moral teaching, whereas traditional Christian moral teaching is constant and not subject to change.

In my view, both implications are destructive to the church and the relationship between church and society. I think that a moral teaching that excels in Don'ts and is rather bleak or wavering on the Dos is neither attractive nor faithful to the Christian mission of being light and salt. Churches that regard the environment of democracy, freedom of expression and separate spheres primarily as a hostile climate in which they need to find a way for traditional moral teaching to survive, aim too low. Why look at these matters in terms of adaptation, convenience, antagonism, retreat or desperate attempts at survival? Why not look at being ahead of it all?

A trajectory of conflict is neither desirable nor viable. The path of constructive engagement with multiple others is more promising. There are always more than two actors on the public stage that actually affect what people believe is right and wrong. Therefore, the analysis of contexts needs to include as many actors as possible. Moreover, it needs to take into account the power play at work between and within the acting organizations. Discussions about moral discourse in and amongst institutions must include an analysis of power issues; otherwise they are not trustworthy.

In the tradition I represent, moral behavior is primarily the fruit of a right relationship with God in Christ, empowered by the spirit. For a communion of churches this implies that celebrating liturgy together as an expression for our need of and our joy in our relationship with God should be a starting point rather than a receipt for achieved uniformity in (moral) teaching.

When conflict between church and state/society is inevitable, the call to resist injustice is both an individual and a communal call. For such resistance to be effective, we need a more dynamic contextualization than one that postulates constant contradiction between church and secularization. We need this because antagonistic frameworks are vastly incapable of dealing with what has become a salient feature of our time: hybridity. In these days, not only human destinies are increasingly marked by hybridity. So is theology, and so are our moral codes. The Declaration of Human Rights and the Convention on the Rights of Children are examples of the hybridity of moral codes; so is the theological discourse on the different uses of the law. One may even say that thanks to the incarnation, hybridity is at the very heart of Christian faith.

The difficulties of the early church in coming to terms with different understandings of the incarnation indicate that hybridity is a more demanding concept to grasp than purity. In fact, it has a tendency to escape one-dimensional definitions. The four particular adverbs of the Chalcedonense are a case in point, as they reflect the struggle for an apt expression of hybridity: two natures, yet without confusion, change, division, or separation (*in duabus naturis inconfuse, immutabiliter, indivise, inseparabiliter*). One may conclude that faithfulness to the Christian tradition may be more about transgressing borders than about defining them. Holy trafficking, if one may say so.

This may also be the clue to a different body economics than the one implied in many exclusive interpretations of the body of Christ.

The people-of-faith-dynamics is a dynamics of overlapping bodies. The exclusive body of Christ is included and permeated by the overlapping loyalty to the body of people of faith—Muslim, Jewish, Buddhist . . .

In light of this, the difference between ecumenism and interfaith dialogue changes character. In light of the new dynamics, ecumenical borders should become like borders within the European Union: no impediments to crossing them.

As unfinished as the concept must be at this point, some consequences are nevertheless quite clear: true politics cannot be confined to the church, contrary to what Cavanaugh, interpreting Augustine, suggests,[22] because true politics and justice cannot do without some kind of subversiveness, which in turn excludes confinement to any one institutional body. This was beautifully illustrated by Martin Marty's observation quoted above: "These churches don't preach politics, but they cannot but be political, because the *polis*, the city, is the arena for the works of God as they interpret and experience them." This also implies that globalization is not necessarily a false catholicity, as assumed by Cavanaugh,[23] because it can in fact go glocal. In this framework, the Eucharist will be considered to be exclusive and at the same time transgressive.

It is a hopeful sign that the statement on interreligious dialogue issued by the Doctrinal commission (läronämnden) of Church of Sweden in 2008[24] will allow for further exploration along these lines.

> Religious traditions have never developed in isolation from each other. They have always interplayed and thus influenced each other. . . . In the encounter with people of different faiths, it is important to strive for knowledge and respect. This is the starting point for a constructive, critical and self-critical dialogue. It is a condition for such dialogue to describe others in a way that they recognize themselves, be mindful of the diversity within the different religions and be willing to share what oneself has found.

---

22. Cavanaugh, *Theopolitical Imagination*, 15.
23. Cavanaugh, *Theopolitical Imagination*, 6.
24. Church of Sweden, *Doctrinal Commission* Statement 2008:6y.

Such dialogue is not only compatible with the faith, confession and teaching of Church of Sweden, but even a way of expressing the faith. It would be strange if Christians would not talk with others who worship God in Sweden.

Such dialogue may also lead to common action—motivated for example by the calling to work for the wellbeing of the city (Jeremiah 29:7) and the view of hospitality (Hebrews 13:2) as a holy duty. These motifs are common to many religious traditions. In certain situations, common action may also include various forms of common prayer.

CONCLUSION

The people-of-faith model is an emerging reality, especially in multicultural and multireligious environments. It cannot yet present the credentials of a long and great history. But it seems to have a potential worth exploring, not only in interfaith dialogue but also as a catalyst for ecclesiological reflections within and between churches. Its main building blocks are the diapractical motifs of hospitality and communal welfare, as well as the will to relate to the other as a positive other as much as possible. It reverses an agenda focused on purity by putting hybridity at the center of attention. In ways yet to explore, this shift resonates with the hybridity that resides at the very center of the Christian gospel: the incarnation in the "hybrid" Jesus Christ. The hybridity expressed through the Chalcedonense can certainly not be a one-to-one blueprint for ecclesiology and interfaith relationships. Nevertheless it invites and maybe even compels us to let go of a purity-driven agenda in favor of further exploring hybridity-driven approaches.

BIBLIOGRAPHY

Adaktusson, Lars. "Det mest försummade kan vara det viktigaste." *Svenska Dagbladet* 16 July (2008).

Ban Ki-moon, Speech. Online: http://www.un.org/News/Press/docs//2007/sgsm11276.doc.htm.

Caputo, John D. *The Weakness of God: A Theology of the Event*. Bloomington & Indianapolis: Indiana University Press, 2006.

Cavanaugh, William T. *Theopolitical Imagination: Discovering the Liturgy as a Political Act in an Age of Global Consumerism*. London, New York: T. & T. Clark, 2002.

Church of Sweden. General Synod. *Doctrinal commission (läronämnden) statement 2008:6y*, August 2008. Online: http://www.svenskakyrkan.se/tcrot/km/2008/betankanden/Ln%202008_06y.shtml#TopOfPage.

FOR THE SAKE OF THE WORLD

Dominus Iesus. Declaration on the Unicity and Salvific Universality of Jesus Christ and the Church, issued by the Congregation for the Doctrine of the Faith of the Roman Catholic Church, 2000. Online: http://www.vatican.va/roman_curia/congregations/cfaith/documents/rc_con_cfaith_doc_20000806_dominus-iesus_en.html.

Dulles, Avery. *Models of the Church*. Expanded Edition. New York et al: Doubleday, 2002 [1974].

Habermas, Jürgen and Joseph Ratzinger. *Dialektik der Säkularisierung*. 7th ed. Freiburg, Basel Wien: Herder, 2007.

Jackelén, Antje. "What is 'Secular'? Techno-Secularism and Spirituality." *Zygon: Journal of Religion and Science*, 40/4 (2005) 863–73.

Jüngel, Eberhard. *Gott als Geheimnis der Welt*. Tübingen: Mohr (Siebeck), 1977.

Kärkkäinen, Veli-Matti. *An Introduction to Ecclesiology*. Downers Grove: InterVarsity, 2002.

Lindgren, Torgny. *Norrlands Akvavit*. Stockholm: Norstedts, 2007.

Marion, Jean-Luc. *God Without Being*. Translated by Thomas A. Carlson. Chicago: University of Chicago Press, 1991.

Marty, Martin E. "Among royalty." In *Christian Century* July 29 (2008) 39.

Robbins, Jeffrey W. "Introduction." In *After the Death of God*, edited by John D. Caputo and Gianni Vattimo. New York: Columbia University Press.

Söderberg, Staffan. "En privatiserad Gud." *Sydsvenskan*, 19 November (2007) B4.

Will, George. "Suicide by Secularism." *Washington Post*, 17 April (2005) B 07.

The Return of the Body

Re-imagining the Ecclesiology of Church of Sweden

OLA SIGURDSON

The Christian church is currently at a crossroads where it has to decide who or what it would like to be in the future, at least in the West. As societies in Europe are becoming more multi-cultural and multi-religious, and as the implicit legal and symbolic contract between church and state—a contract that has been in place at least since the Westphalian peace treaty from 1648—is being re-negotiated as a consequence of this, the way forward for Christian churches of all denominations necessarily implies a re-imagining of their identities. This is true, of course, for the majority churches, which have been in the position of defining religious observance in their respective nation-state, but it is true for the minority or free churches (or any other religious communities) as well, as far as they have been identified and have identified themselves in contrast to the majority church of their respective state. If there is some truth in Hegel's sentence from his *Rechtsphilosophie* that Minerva's owl only flies at dusk, and I think there is, the task of theology is to interpret this change, re-describing the identity of the church in a more fruitful way, and this is what I think is being done, however tentatively and searching, in this volume.

My task, in this final chapter, has been to relate the six previous chapters to one another—"to get them on speaking terms with one another" as the editor of this volume, Jonas Ideström, has put it in his introduction. This means putting them in some kind of interpretative context that they hypothetically might not recognize as their own. Some mild form of hermeneutical violence has thus been the condition of possibility for completing this task. I hope that the different authors may think that the context I give might at least be worth its while to disagree with—in other words, that they might be, even after this chapter, on speaking terms with me. The hypothesis that structures this chapter is that all authors in this volume in different ways reason about the return of the body. To achieve my task, I shall begin with a section where I explain how I understand the return of the body, or, perhaps better, the new visibility of the social embodiment of Church of Sweden and the historical—political and theological—processes that has led to this new visibility. Against this background I then proceed to analyze what I see as the common thread of the volume in three sections, beginning with William Cavanaugh and the question of church and/or state as organic wholes, continuing with Arne Rasmusson and Henrik Widmark on embodiment, practices and space and finishing with Ninna Edgardh, Göran Gunner and Antje Jackelén on the more political and social implications of this return of the body. I end my chapter with some short remarks on topics for further reflection on such a quest for the re-description of the identity of the church.

THE NEW VISIBILITY OF SOCIAL EMBODIMENT

The main focus of this volume has been on my own church, Church of Sweden, a church that has organized religion in Sweden since "Uppsala möte" in 1593, which marks the consolidation of the Swedish nation-state as of Lutheran confession. Even though religious minorities of different kinds have existed within the Swedish kingdom in between 1593 and 2000, when Church of Sweden became disestablished and the contract was dissolved at least in juridical terms, the territory of the kingdom of Sweden was officially declared as Lutheran in confession in accordance with the principle *cuius regio, eius religio*, i.e.: that the religion of the people of the nation follows its king or leader. In the period of the rise of the nation-state, religion corresponded in principle to nationality and thus to a certain territory. The body politic and the social embodiment of the church became one and the same.

At least since the dawn of Swedish modernity in the 1920s, this contract has coexisted with the gradual secularization of Swedish society. It is sometimes put forward as a thesis that Sweden or Scandinavia or Northern Europe is one of the most secularized parts of the world, but the truth of such a contention depends on what you mean by secularization and also how and where you look. It is surely true that Sweden has been secularized in the sense of the diminishing formal political power of Church of Sweden. In the terms of José Casanova's three-dimensions of secularization, Sweden—as well as Europe as a whole—has been secularized in the sense that "religion" has been differentiated from "economy" and "politics" and "culture" so as to constitute its own autonomous sphere.[1] It could also be said that it has been secularized in the sense of an increasing privatization, but with this dimension one should perhaps be a bit more careful; if one means a decreasing church attendance at Sunday mass during the last part of the twentieth century, it is true. And if one means by privatization that religion is more and more being seen as the "choice" of a "consumer" that now has the option of picking out his or her "preferences" on the "religious smorgasbord" without regard for any church or religion subsidized by the state, it is probably also true. But if one means the complete individualization of religion, I am not so sure. There might be reason to think that the religious communities that are being formed do not fit into the traditional dichotomy private/public, at least when anything that does not belong to the state is defined as private. New circumstances form new communities or social embodiments or even make some social embodiments (even traditional religious bodies such as Church of Sweden) visible in a new way. If Sweden is a secularized country, it has increasingly been recognized that the version of secularity which has characterized Sweden has been very Lutheran.

As for Casanova's third dimension, the disappearance of religion, in continuity with the foregoing I would say that what has happened in Sweden is rather the transformation of religion than its disappearance. It is certainly an open question whether Sweden in any other sense than historical could or should be called a Christian nation-state, but answering that question in the negative does not mean that Sweden today is a non-religious nation. Sweden, I would suggest, is now a more visible multi-religious society than it was just some decades ago. This new plurality, cultural and religious, defines the context for the search for a new identity for the Christian church in Sweden but also, of course, for Swedish society as a whole. That the bond between church and state has been loosened

---

1. Casanova, *Public Religions*, 19–39.

is an important event in principle, as an adaptation on behalf of both church and society to a multi-religious social reality.

To see why this situation implies a new visibility and a re-imagining of the social embodiment of the church in Sweden, we need to make a little detour into the effective history of the Lutheran doctrine of the two kingdoms.[2] One of the features of this history is that the doctrine has come to contribute to the development of the modern distinction between religion and politics and the subsequent privatization of faith in European modernity. In a very general form, this doctrine distinguishes between the realm of the "outward human being" and the "inner human being," where the "outward human being" is a citizen in the worldly and political realm and the "inner human being" is a citizen in the spiritual and private realm. Both the worldly and the spiritual realm is ruled by God, but whereas the worldly realm is God's rule over every human being irrespective of faith through God's law, enacted through the force of worldly political authorities, the spiritual realm is the realm of faith governed by the gospel of God's forgiveness through Christ. Of course, it could well be argued that Martin Luther himself never intended that his occasional writings about the relationship between the two kingdoms should take up the position of doctrine, but nevertheless this is how these writings effectively have functioned in the process of modernization of European Lutheran nation-states. The effect of this separation between the outer and the inner has come to be a part of a wider set of distinctions in modernity between the body and the voice, the worldly and the spiritual, the rational and the emotive, the active and the passive, the masculine and the feminine and so on.

These distinctions have had fatal consequences for the self-understanding of the Christian church in the ongoing process of modernization from the absolutistic, confessional state to the liberal and more non-confessional state: when the government withdraws from its theological self-understanding and the worldly realm becomes radically secularized, religion becomes a private, passive and feminine sentiment. In other words, religion looses any notion of its institutional character; in William Cavanaugh's words from his chapter in this volume, its "vocation to wholeness"; it becomes subjectivized to the degree that it looses its body, its particularity and its place. It is not only that it has become 'a separate

---

2. Cf. Henriksen, "Pluralism and Identity," 277–90.

enclave that stands apart from and judges the world from without'; the loss of any identifiable embodiment means that it cannot even stand apart from anything else except through a particular set of doctrines or moral principles.

What this means is of course not that the social embodiment of the Christian church has disappeared in the social sense. Any given parish functions through a set of practices that together constitute a social embodiment; the liturgy is celebrated, deacons help the needy, people are gathered to study the bible, day care for small children and choirs are being organized, et cetera. But what it means is that this embodied or social embodiment in all its ordinariness is not seen as something integral to the theological understanding of faith but rather as something external. Together with the central doctrine of Lutheran theology that the church is a *creatura Verbi*, i.e. a creation of the Word as mediated by preaching, this has worked towards an understanding of faith as something that is "inner" in contrast to what is merely "outward." What is outward is just an external tool for authentic, inner faith and so could be administered as something purely contingent and secular that could be used for other purposes as well, such as the cohesion of the nation-state. My father once told me that my grandfather was a churchwarden and my grandmother a believer. This, I have come to realize, is a good illustration of the effective division of the two kingdoms in Sweden; my grandfather's position did not have anything particular to do with what he believed (or not) but with his position in the local community where he was a relatively prosperous farmer. Belief was, so to speak, left to the women, to the private and the socially inconsequential.

Today, compared to the middle of the last century, this dichotomization of the two kingdoms has developed further until they have fallen apart altogether. If yesterday the social embodiment of the Christian church came to be identified with the body politic of the nation-state through the territorialisation of religion, in today's plural society it is obvious—even for neo-integralists who wish to realign nation and religion—that the ecclesial body and the body of the state are two and different. Carl Schmitt's "typically Judeo-Christian division of the original political unity" has again become visible when church and state have been separated and religion has become de-territorialized.[3] If yesterday the relative religious

3. Schmitt, *Leviathan*, 10.

homogeneity of a particular European nation-state made the distinction between church and state a distinction *within* its particular body politic, today the relative religious heterogeneity of the same nation-state makes it obvious that one has to distinguish between *different* modes of social embodiment. One could count several reasons for this—the erosion of traditional religion from within, immigration, globalization, et cetera. One way to state what has happened, however, is that the church that for some hundred years has been considered identical with the Swedish state through this identification has become almost invisible because taken for granted as the normal state of things. But through the increasing religious plurality, the disestablishment of the state church-system and the relative secularization in late modern Sweden, even Church of Sweden is no more an invisible presupposition. Other forms of social embodiment that compete or even conflict with the social embodiment of Church of Sweden, make the body of Church of Sweden visible anew, even to itself, as a distinct body that (no longer) is identical to the body of the Swedish society. This, in turn, has several consequences, but just to mention one that has importance for this volume: the separation of church and state necessarily implies that the question of the relationship between religion and politics comes up again—if, that is, religion has not been thoroughly privatized—something that the chapters in this book hopefully have made clear.

The reason for talking about the change that is happening as a new visibility is, I would assume, that this marks the continuity with what has come before. The kind of "folk church" theology—in several different and conflicting versions—that has characterized the ecclesiology of Church of Sweden may not be an option any more, but that does not mean that everything that this particular church has said or done no longer has any theological legitimacy. What the new situation calls for is what I above termed a re-description of the identity of the church in a, for the contemporary context, more fruitful way. One lack I have identified above is a theology of social embodiment that does not identify the body politic of the nation-state with the body of Christ but recognizes the distinction between the two. Having a sense of one's own body means being aware of its limits. In words from the memoir of the British philosopher Gillian Rose: "A soul which is not bound is as mad as one with cemented boundaries."[4] So, for the church to regain some theologically legitimate conception of

---

4. Rose, *Love's Work*, 98.

its social embodiment is not a case for ecclesial exclusivism—a critique sometimes heard against the kind of re-description of the church that this volume suggests—but rather a case against the kind of ecclesiology that in its inclusivism has no sense of the limits of the church and therefore never really gets to meet the other as other. The return of the body means the return of the other's body as well and vice-versa

CHURCH AND/OR STATE AS ORGANIC WHOLES?

William T. Cavanaugh has recently emerged as one of the more perceptive contemporary theologians dealing with ecclesiology. It is truly beneficial to have his reflections on the Swedish context. His chapter begins with the statement that it is impossible to "do ecclesiology in the abstract, free of context." I could not agree more, and my own introduction to this final chapter has perhaps also shown my agreement in practice. Cavanaugh makes it very clear that his own perspective is Catholic and North American rather than Lutheran or Swedish and so his contribution is that of an outsider. I do not view this as a case of false modesty, but rather as an important hermeneutical point; his view is not a view from nowhere but from somewhere else in regard to church and society in Sweden. This view from somewhere else allows him to see things in the context under discussion in this volume that might not be visible to a native such as me.

One interesting point of view on Swedish modernity, is Cavanaugh's comparison of it to Carl Schmitt's notion of an organic state. From my own point of view, I would not see an immediate historical continuity between Rudolf Kjellén's conception of the state (that is being compared to Schmitt) and later representatives of the Swedish modernity. Kjellén was a conservative politician and also one of the early adopters of the expression "folkhemmet," later appropriated by social democratic politician Per Albin Hansson in a famous speech in 1928 (the expression still has rich, if somewhat nostalgic connotations in Swedish culture). Kjellén was also the father-in-law of the priest and church leader Manfred Björkquist, who used the expression in 1912 apropos the national subscription in aid of a new armoured cruiser.

The kind of organic view of the state that Kjellén represented was, however, severely criticized as 'metaphysics' by such prominent Swedish thinkers as political theorist and editor-in-chief Herbert Tingsten and professor of economics Gunnar Myrdal. If there were any constructors of the Swedish model, they surely were among them.[5] But they would have nothing to do with anything called an organic view of the state. The state, according to them, was just a conglomerate of individuals, at least methodologically. Tingsten, the liberal of the two, claimed that such metaphysics caused disunity in a people, but fortunately, after the Second World War, every metaphysical world-view was on the wane, and you could claim that Sweden, the Swedish model, was what he called "*en lycklig demokrati*" (almost untranslatable: perhaps "a happy democracy" but better "*eine gluckliche Demokratie*"). Among the arch-enemy's of both Myrdal and Tingsten were organic conceptions of the state.

I would therefore say that Kjellén has not been such an important influence for Swedish modernity, but that Cavanaugh's chapter still is perceptive in its characterization of Sweden. Even though Tingsten and Myrdal refused anything "metaphysical," they still claimed that Sweden was a very homogeneous society where the state had an important duty to actively cultivate this homogeneity. The term "folkhemmet", used by the social democratic prime minister Per Albin (he is usually referred to by his first name only, even in public prose, as he was regarded as a kind of father of his people), suggests that Sweden was regarded as a "home," which implies a family, rather than as a railway station or a warehouse, and so as some kind of organic whole. Despite themselves, both Tingsten and Myrdal also had a view of society that very well could be analyzed by the political theory of Carl Schmitt as it has everything to do with sovereignty and national unity. Just to mention one quote where Tingsten applauds the Swedish quest for homogeneity that shows how this organic unity is actively cultivated:

> When the Swedish and Danish kings four hundred years ago, protected by a relative isolation, exterminated [*sic!*] one of the main positions of Christianity, Catholicism, they promoted the founding of one of the world's most accomplished communities.[6]

An organic view of the state is actively promoted but at the same time and in many ways unacknowledged. I think this quote highlights one of the main reasons for the trouble Sweden has in becoming a more pluralistic

---

5. Cf. Sigurdson, *Den lyckliga filosofin*.
6. Tingsten, *Från idéer till idyll*, 9f.

society: the unacknowledged but actively promoted homogeneity. There is a silent presupposition that conflict is a thing of the past, and so anyone who wishes to disagree with the national consensus on how things are and how the state should be governed is almost pathologized. Sweden is in this way of thinking, long before the current political debate, the paradise of post-politics, the model of what Ulrich Beck calls a "simple" in contrast to a "reflexive" modernity[7]—or one is tempted to say that Swedish modernity in fact if not in theory was pre-modern rather than modern. In such a cultural climate, neither the Christian church nor any other religious institution could be allowed to have a public voice of its own that potentially could come into conflict with the voice of the state or of the "people." Thus, religion became privatized and invisible, rather than a quest for wholeness. As Cavanaugh points out, even a welfare state makes a claim "to embrace the wholeness of the lives of its citizens" and so the church, as the weaker party to the contract between church and state, seems to be faced with the alternative of either identifying with the aspiration of the welfare state or becoming privatized and spiritualized.

Cavanaugh suggests, with the help of both the Catholic theologian Henri de Lubac and the Reformed theologian Karl Barth, that the Christian church as a "catholic" church (in the ecumenical, not the confessional, sense) necessarily aspires to wholeness. This means, for Cavanaugh, "the integration of all of life in one place into a coherent whole." I would agree, but only on the presumption that one does not forget what Cavanaugh also claims with the help of Carl Schmitt, namely, that Christianity has also stood for a rupture of organic wholeness, the "typically Judeo-Christian division of the original political unity." For good reasons, his chapter is entitled "Separation *and* Wholeness." On the political side, what the development of late modernity has meant is a rupture of the identification of the national and the ecclesial body. As the ecclesial body starts to become visible again in its separation from the state, it begins a process of re-appropriation of its own social embodiment. This is a process to affirm, but, and this is a question in the wake of Cavanaugh's chapter, how should this process avoid the establishment of an organic wholeness on the part of the church that claims for itself an absolute status that only pertains to God? Is there not an obvious risk that this leads to a new, territorially defined, social body that forgets that

7. Beck, *Risk Society*.

the city of God and the city of men could not be joined together until the *eschaton*? Is there not a risk with any conception of organic wholeness, at least if it intends to be pure?

I guess I nourish a Lutheran worry about the (in my eyes all too visible) fallibility or sinfulness of the concrete church, regardless of denomination, to be altogether comfortable with any such talk of "organic wholeness," be it on behalf of the church or the state. Cavanaugh discusses the dialectic between separation and wholeness all through his chapter, and I am in agreement with most of his historical descriptions, also with his characterization of the failure of Reformation when it comes to the political relation between church and state. At the very end, he writes on the one hand about the "unsettling political presence of Christ's rule in the world" through the church and on the other hand about how "the church's vocation to wholeness means that it cannot become a separate enclave that stands apart from and judges the world from without." What I would want to discuss in more detail with Cavanaugh is two things: First, what the sinfulness of the church—which Cavanaugh acknowledges, for sure—means for the understanding of its embodiment. Is it not necessary to speak more emphatically of the "split between the *already* and the *not yet* of the Kingdom of God" as a "political split," *but also* as "a split that runs through every individual Christian" *and* through every social embodiment? Even if the Reformation is one of the factors that contributed to the disappearance of the social embodiment of the church in privatizing the split, is there still not some truth in the Reformation's critique of the sinful church, a church where the split runs through every individual church, together with the rest of the world? Second, does not the—in some sense—provisional existence of the church before the *eschaton* call for a more thorough discussion about *what kind of embodiment* that is the condition of existence for the church still on its way? I would suggest that the Russian linguist Mikhail Bakhtin's distinction between a "finished" and "classical" body and a grotesque "body in the act of becoming" would help us to distinguish between different modes of embodiments and so of wholeness as something also "in the act of becoming" rather than as something already accomplished.[8] This is nothing I believe I say against

---

8. Bakhtin, *Rabelais and His World*, 320. I have developed this line of thought in my article "The Christian Body as a Grotesque Body," but also, at further length, in *Himmelska kroppar*, chapters 9 and 11.

Cavanaugh's chapter, merely something I believe is necessary to pursue in the wake of his excellent discussion of the separation of church and state and the consequences for the aspiration of wholeness of the church through history.

EMBODIMENT, PRACTICES AND SPACE

But what does it mean to reclaim the social embodiment of a particular church as, for instance, Church of Sweden? In his contribution to this volume, "Sacrament as social process," Arne Rasmusson has put it succinctly with the help of Mennonite theologian John Howard Yoder: "It is common practices that constitute the church as a social body." These practices are nothing wildly esoteric but rather ordinary, public practices that the church believes God is acting "in, with and under." Examples of such practices given by Yoder and discussed by Rasmusson are baptism, breaking bread, fraternal admonition, the universality of charisma and the Spirit's freedom in the meeting. Far from being an exhaustive list, it could be supplemented in various ways, according to ecclesial tradition. But the examples mentioned by Rasmusson are probably, for almost any ecclesial tradition, "central Christian social practices" and so part of the constitution of the social embodiment of the church. These practices, in all their variety, are not something external to faith but integral to the theological understanding of Christian existence.

Now, Yoder was a Mennonite theologian, and this is also the tradition from which Rasmusson writes. Thus, it comes as no surprise that Rasmusson's chapter contains some critical remarks on how these practices have fared under the system of state Christendom. In the beginning of his chapter, Rasmusson with Yoder claims that baptism is a social process that incorporates a person in the body of Christ and relativizes all other identities. But in Christendom, baptism has come to stand for incorporation into the nation-state, as its territory has been identified with a particular confession: "After the Reformation, baptism became increasingly incorporation into a national body." The national body became the primary body—and as I have suggested above, in line with Rasmusson's argument, the ecclesial body and the national body were identified. The sacrament was now distinguished from the social process, and so the presence of God was so to speak divorced from the practices as such. Rasmusson's suggestion, in his chapter, is the need to return to an understanding of sacraments as social processes so as to counter the detrimental effects of Protestantism in European and global history having become "the midwife of modern nationalism." This particular temptation to align itself with nationalism has not, for obvious reasons, been a possibility for a Radical Reformation church such as the Mennonite church. Such a church has always had to define its social embodiment in relation to other bodies and has never run the risk of suggesting that its possible organic wholeness contains both church and state. Perhaps a Mennonite church rather has had to fight the opposite temptation, namely to exist as (in Cavanaugh's words) "a separate enclave that stands apart from and judges the world from without." Be that as it may for now, what Mennonite and other Radical Reformation churches contribute to the current discussion of ecclesiology is a perspective from a very different relationship to the nation-state and a different mode of embodiment.

The point of Rasmusson's chapter is not that the churches of the Radical Reformation consist of practices, whereas the traditional Protestant Reformation did not. But it is an argument against the spiritualization of the sacraments, so that their social dimensions become theologically external. Such a practice as baptism is not, in itself, self-interpreting, which means that it could be put to more or less benign use. Rasmusson's Mennonite perspective is a critical perspective that needs to be heard in a church such as Church of Sweden, but even beside that, his chapter also contains an outline of the kind of ecclesiological redescription that could clarify any discussion of what Church of Sweden would want to be today. The editor of this volume, Jonas Ideström, has in his dissertation *Lokal kyrklig identitet* analyzed what he calls the "implicit ecclesiology" of the "local identity of the church" through a case-study of the practices and discourses of the parish church of Flemingsberg.[9] This contextual analysis shows the fruitfulness of the kind of approach that Rasmusson's chapter suggests even for analyzing and discussing the ecclesiology of Church of Sweden.

A further contribution to such an approach could be found in Henrik Widmark's chapter on Church of Sweden and the social segregation of Rosengård. This chapter is a very profound argument that employs several different theories of culture to re-describe a particular ecclesial event, namely the withdrawal of the church from a socially segregated

---

9. Ideström, *Lokal kyrklig identitet*.

part of Sweden—and how this has consequences for the future of this very district in Malmö. "To leave is a decision—with consequences; it is a statement willingly or unwillingly—it is a political act." As Church of Sweden, for reasons that by now probably are familiar, is identified with traditional Swedish society, the de-consecration if its local church cannot but be understood as Swedish society leaving Rosengård to its destiny. That this ecclesial act is a significant political act is a fact that could, of course, be made to disappear with the help of a certain ecclesiology that defines its parish in terms of two-dimensional territory. As the territory of Rosengård formally belongs to the parish of Västra Skrävlinge, a certain kind of ecclesiology, indifferent to the social processes that actually make up the symbolic spaces that human beings inhabit, could claim that Church of Sweden still is present in Rosengård even if it has no particular material, embodied presence there. In a two-dimensional cartographic model, the Church of Sweden could be said to be present in each and every corner of Sweden, as the territory of the nation-state is being divided up with the help of a map. What Widmark accomplishes in his chapter is to show how another mapping that is three- rather than two-dimensional gives us a completely different understanding of the social presence of the church. Three-dimensional in contrast to two-dimensional necessarily implies a focus on the body and the social embodiment of the church as an institution. Widmark mentions, in a section on the territorial church, how the "historical Church of Sweden was formed as a part of the building of a nation and a civil society" and how this understanding remains despite the fact that "today, society is organized and understood differently." In the case of the material and symbolic discrepancy between the multi-cultural district Rosengård and the more traditional parish Västra Skrävlinge, this means that a two-dimensional territorial understanding of the presence of the church is not very helpful, to put it mildly. The future for Rosengård is bleak, according to Widmark: "the only thing that holds the residents together is estrangement from Swedish society."

A question for further ecclesiological exploration in line with Widmark's mode of thought would be whether the system of territorial parishes might be a reason for the relative neglect of the notion of the church as the body of Christ in the history of ecclesiology in Sweden. Another question would be whether the focus on place rather than space might contribute to the spiritualization of the church as, to quote

Widmark, "buildings are just buildings and can be treated as a financial matter." Financial, that is, not theological, belonging to the "outward human being" rather than the "inner human being." A further question, also proposed by Widmark's chapter, is whether the category of space is more open to plurality, as it can contain coexisting but distinct trajectories, whereas place, at least in the European nation-state, suggests a drift towards homogeneity, as distinct trajectories necessarily would mean conflicting trajectories. I mention these questions here, not as a prelude to an attempt to answer them, but as an example of how a re-description—this time with the help of some prominent theoreticians of space—generates new questions that help to illuminate the current situation as well as to re-imagining the church. It is interesting to note, finally, that Widmark's chapter also could be said to make use of the notion of embodiment in his attempt to re-describe the identity of the church, as almost all chapters in this volume. My suggestion is, again, that this has to do with the new visibility of the social embodiment of the church.

Both Rasmusson and Widmark give a rather bleak picture of the practices of Church of Sweden. In a more general historical account of the social practices that together make up the particular body of Church of Sweden, one would probably come to realize that some of these practices conflict with others. Picturing the church as a body does not mean that all practices work towards the same *telos*. Again, the notion of the church as an organic whole might mislead us to believe that an institution such as Church of Sweden is a smoothly working organ with all its parts moving in the same direction. Given the very real conflicts not only in between social embodiments but also internal in any given social embodiment, it is hardly a question of either/or. Perhaps Protestantism was not *only* "the midwife of modern nationalism" but also, at least partly, the midwife of modern democracy. The Reformation idea that anyone was allowed to read their Bible implied the ability to do so, and so was instrumental in developing the common ability to read. My point is not that Rasmusson necessarily is wrong in his characterization of Protestantism as the "the midwife of modern nationalism." I just want to claim that these historical processes are complex and so one might find practices, even in majority traditions such as Church of Sweden, that imply something more or different than nationalism. There might also be cases of practices that contribute to a more fruitful self-understanding of the church today. These practices are likely to become more visible as Church of Sweden grows out of its dependence on the Swedish nation-state and begins to re-imagine itself, perhaps with the help of Mennonite as well as Catholic ecclesiology and also cultural theory.

THE POLITICS OF PRACTICE

Ninna Edgardh's and Göran Gunner's chapters, on the church and welfare and on human rights, respectively, both concern the social embodiment of the church. A focus on social embodiment means, with necessity, as it seems, a church that is more explicitly political. Being a *social* embodiment implies having some idea of how life together shall be realized. Not being a state church anymore, Church of Sweden might plausibly have the possibility of playing a much more constructive political role than before just by being the church and not a part of the state administration. The disestablishment of the church from the state may liberate the church so that it could play a more independent and relevant role, without pretending or feeling obliged to speak for everyone or mimic the voice of the state, as a part of what has been called the prophetic mission of the church. In the words of the cultural theorist Michel de Certeau, a church that is not in the place of being a hegemonical religion in a certain nation has no possibility of being "strategic," as it does not possess any place from where it can create the necessary overview.[10] Instead, it has to develop a "tactic," which does not count on having its own home territory but has to react in creative ways, "making do" with whatever hand the circumstances deal it.

Edgardh's idea of the church having a "queer role" in its being a social agent lends itself very easily to what I have called a re-description and a re-imagining of the identity of the church. Her point is lifting up the importance of the social practice that concerns itself with care giving and concern for marginalized human beings in a time when efficiency and self-fulfillment have become the norm. This practice has, both then and now, more often than not, been carried on by women, but has often been "belittled, even by the churches themselves and referred to inferior sectors separated from the more highly valued sectors of liturgy and dogmatics." This practice, in its very ordinariness, is today a very queer practice, at least compared to prevailing standards. Edgardh uses the metaphor of

10. Certeau, *The Practice of Everyday Life*, xix.

the "invisible hand" in a sense rather different from Adam Smith's when she claims that the condition of possibility of being an autonomous agent depends on "the existence of invisible hands reaching out to those who cannot live up to the ideal"—and she could well have continued with the importance of these invisible hands for nurturing this agent through infancy and adolescence before it becomes autonomous. Those "invisible hands," she claims, "most often are hands of women"—and this is due to historical reasons that involve the role of religion, gender and care-giving in late modernity. "Invisible hands"—invisible in the same sense, I would suggest, that the social embodiment has been invisible. And if we do not see the hands that catch us when we fall before we fall, it may be that they have disappeared due to not being acknowledged.

Edgardh practices, in her chapter, the art of "looking awry" at a given object and thus seeing a strange but distinct pattern that tells another story than the usual. If this has been the historical role of women, perhaps it is time to recognize how this practice is important, and perhaps not only important but absolutely central, to any church that wishes to be the church of Christ? Perhaps it is more central today than ever, given the negative development of the welfare state in Europe? The point is not to defend the continuation of a gendered practice, so that women should continue with their serving and men with the often more comfortable tasks of dogmatics and liturgy, but rather the re-evaluation of what has been going on all the time, unacknowledged, and the remaining need for care-giving practices in today's societies. The point is neither to argue against the modern ideal of the autonomous agent but to, in the words of another queer philosopher, Judith Butler,

> qualify that claim through recourse to the fundamental sociality of embodied life, the ways in which we are, from the start and by virtue of being a bodily being, already given over, beyond ourselves, implicated in lives that are not our own.[11]

The return to tradition is not an attempt to validate gender inequality—on the contrary—but still to use tradition to question some things taken for granted in late modernity. Edgardh uses queer theology to re-describe a certain practice that has been going on for hundreds or thousands of years, basically saying that this practice is needed now, but it has always

---

11. Butler, *Precarious Life*, 28.

been needed but has been so self-evident as to become almost invisible. This is an example of how it is possible to find historical practices that help us to re-imagine the church in a more fruitful way in light of contemporary circumstances and also an example of, as alluded to in the previous section, how there are ecclesial practices that have existed all along but that might have gone against the grain of other practices. What Edgardh reminds us of is actually the very central practice of *diakonia*. That there is a need to remind us of the centrality of this practice is in itself a sign that something has been lacking in the implementation of ecclesiology.

Gunner, in his chapter "She Keeps Bothering Me," also discusses the church as a social embodiment, or, in his own words, "a community of addressed participants." This community has an important responsibility for human rights in being an intermediary institution between the individual and the state. The church, in other words, is an actor in civil society. In the recent debate on human rights it has been suggested that the traditional focus on the state as bearing the sole responsibility for the implementation of these rights is not sufficient, given that the state often rejects them in theory or practice. The church could function as a community of empowerment for people whose rights have been violated and the human rights language could offer the church a language for taking into account solidarity with the needy, the suffering and the oppressed. Gunner's suggestion is not that the church could be reduced to a human rights organization but that its message about the arrival of the Kingdom of God has affinities with the vision of human rights.

One important trajectory in Gunner's chapter, that he also shares with the other authors in this volume, is to overcome the division between public and private. I think this theme is connected to what I have suggested above about the new visibility of social embodiment. A church such as Church of Sweden is no longer a part of state government but still not reducible to the private sphere if by that one means something purely individual. It might be hard to show here how the configuration of Swedish modernity tended to inflate the distinction between state and society, but let me just suggest that the disestablishment of churches in Europe is a part of a process that includes the increasing recognition of the plurality of society (even in Sweden). The idea of a central government has, if not replaced, then at least been complemented by the recognition that political decision always has to be implemented by intermediary institutions and that these institutions play a decisive role in how these decisions are mediated and also could stand in conflict with the central government. The church is a part of this intermediary structure but plays a different role than business companies and financial institutions in having its own internal motivation for caring for the needy and the oppressed. The church could, like the woman in Luke 18:1–8, go on being troublesome and bother the authorities day and night about the situation of the suffering within and without its own limits, as every human being is created in the image of God. Human rights are a part of the church's struggle for justice. What seems to be implied in Gunner's suggestion is that to play this part in society, the church has to accept its non-governmental role or, in other words, recognize itself as a visible body distinct from the national body once again.

It is interesting to note that both Edgardh's and Gunner's chapters relate the church's mission for justice to quite modern values such as welfare and human rights in a time when modernity, perhaps, is becoming fragmented. Of course it is possible to speak about both welfare and human rights in a certain sense even before modernity, but it is obvious from their respective discussions that it is with the modern values of welfare and human rights that they are concerned. This shows, among other things, that church and modernity hardly could be envisioned as each other's opposites and that there might be a certain religious core of modernity that the church might want to defend when modernity is under attack.[12] And so Antje Jackelén's comment in her chapter, that the "Swedish welfare systems reveal traits of secularized Christianity, especially in the shape of the Lutheran tradition," is indirectly confirmed by both Edgardh and Gunner. Maybe secular Sweden never was so secular after all, maybe its particular form of religiosity just was too taken for granted to be visible as such? The "return of religion," which is the topic of Jackelén's chapter, also concerns itself with the notion of social embodiment—"a different kind of body economy" as her subtitle states it. This "different kind of body economy" includes the recognition that the church hardly any longer is located at the center of society and that an ecclesial vision oriented towards a consumer model just is not enough. She also questions, in the light of the multireligious experience of contemporary society, how one shall speak of the social embodiment of the church in a way that does justice to this situa-

---

12. Cf. Gillespie, *Theological Origins of Modernity*.

tion. Her own suggestion is that it makes more sense to speak of hybridity than of purity. Different traditions—different social embodiments—always intermingle, and this has been accentuated by the experience of multi-culturalism. This hybridity is not just something that is imposed on the Christian church from outside of its own tradition, but a creative consequence of the incarnation where humanity and divinity meet and intermingle. This gives us the conceptual space for understanding how interfaith dialogue is possible. Thus, she is more keen than Cavanaugh to emphasize that "true politics cannot be confined to the church." I recognize in her chapter some of my—perhaps Lutheran—worries about how the fallibility or sinfulness of the concrete church comes to the fore in the talk of the organic wholeness of the church. Here I think it needs to be spelt out more clearly how this "dynamics of overlapping bodies" works so as to avoid the impression that we get the old hegemonical state church of modernity in return, just re-named "the body of people-of-faith." Is not the talk of "hybridity" all too well tuned in to the free-floating economy of late modern capitalism? But at the same time, Jackelén also shares with Cavanaugh and the other authors in this volume the recognition of the end of the state church-system, the new visibility of a distinct (if not pure) social embodiment of the church and of the inevitable political impact of any social embodiment, including Church of Sweden. Jackelén identifies a topic that hardly is a minor concern for any ecclesiology reflecting on today's society, namely how to live together with people belonging to different social embodiments. A church that is no longer at the center of society, that no longer has any claims to religious hegemony or at least no power to enforce such hegemony, is a church that has recognized that it is not alone, that its particular mode of embodiment also means the ability to meet the other through its very limits.

CONCLUDING REMARKS

The hypothesis that has structured this chapter is that all authors in different ways reason about the return of the body. They are all concerned that the social embodiment of the church should once again become something integral to the theological understanding of the church. The re-imagining and re-description that I would like to see, and which I interpret these chapters being a part of, is in part caused by historical processes that the church—whether Church of Sweden nor any other church—cannot control. To me it is obvious that any such re-imagining has to be contextually informed, which means also historically informed, and does not begin from scratch. But the church is not the external bystander, regarding these processes from the roadside, so to speak, but can always choose a more active role—if not strategic then tactical—even if it never can predict how its particular actions and reactions are going to work out in practice. This is also why ecclesiology never could be done 'from above', without regard for the empirical church, except in the hermeneutical meaning that there always is the possibility to use theory to perceive and understand the empirical church more deeply—as done eminently well by both William Cavanaugh and Henrik Widmark in this volume. When Church of Sweden and the Swedish state divorced each other in the beginning of the new century, I was worried that the reflection on the church after the divorce mainly concerned itself with matters of law and organization. Perhaps that is what happens just after a divorce, but to find itself anew the church also needs to reflect on its own identity (identity in the sense of being someone in a relationship rather than having some sort of static essence). The alternative is alienation and disorientation. Thus, all the chapters in this volume have made me happy, not only for the answers they give in what I perceive is a common theme, the return of the body, but also for the questions they have generated as a challenge to take this investigation and the quest for the re-imagining of the church even further. Among these I once again would like to mention the nature of embodiment, the question of place and space and the impact of a particular social embodiment such as the Christian church in a multi-religious society. The British literary theorist and critic Terry Eagleton has recently claimed that theology is "one of the most ambitious theoretical arenas left in an increasingly specialized world."[13] I believe that the authors with whom I have had the pleasure to discuss in this concluding chapter, testify to the truth of that claim, not least in the questions they generate.

BIBLIOGRAPHY

Bakhtin, Mikhail. *Rabelais and His World*. Translated by Helene Iswolsky. Cambridge, Mass./London: The M.I.T. Press, 1968.

---

13. Eagleton, "Culture & Barbarism," 14.

Beck, Ulrich. *Risk Society: Towards a New Modernity*. Translated by Mark Ritter. London: Sage, 1992.
Butler, Judith. *Precarious Life: The Power of Mourning and Violence*. London/New York: Verso, 2004.
Casanova, José, *Public Religions in the Modern World*. Chicago/London: The University of Chicago Press, 1994.
de Certeau, Michel. *The Practice of Everyday Life*. Translated by Steven Randall. Berkeley: The University of California Press, 1984.
Eagleton, Terry. "Culture & Barbarism: Metaphysics in the Time of Terror." *Commonweal: A Review of Religion, Politics and Culture*, Volume CXXXVI, Number 6 (2009) 9–14.
Gillespie, Michael Allen. *The Theological Origins of Modernity*. Chicago: The University of Chicago Press, 2008.
Henriksen, Jan-Olav. "Pluralism and Identity: The Two-Kingdoms Doctrine Challenged by Secularization and Privatization." In *The Gift of Grace: The Future of Lutheran Theology*, edited by Niels Henrik Gregersen et al., 277–90. Minneapolis: Fortress, 2005.
Ideström, Jonas. *Lokal kyrklig identitet: En studie av implicit ecklesiologi med exemplet Svenska kyrkan i Flemingsberg*. Skellefteå: Artos, 2009.
Rose, Gillian. *Love's Work*. London: Chatto & Windus, 1995.
Schmitt, Carl. *The Leviathan in the State Theory of Thomas Hobbes: Meaning and Failure of a Political Symbol*. Translated by George Schwab and Erna Hilfstein. Westport, CT: Greenwood, 1996.
Sigurdson, Ola. *Den lyckliga filosofin: Etik och politik hos Hägerström, Tingsten, makarna Myrdal och Hedenius*. Stockholm/Stehag: Brutus Östllings bokförlag Symposion, 2000.
———. *Himmelska kroppar: Inkarnation, blick, kroppslighet*. Logos/Pathos 6. Göteborg: Glänta, 2006.
———. "The Christian Body as a Grotesque Body." In *Embodiment in Cognition and Culture*, edited by John Michael Krois et al., 243–58. Amsterdam: John Benjamins, 2007.
Tingsten, Herbert. *Från idéer till idyll: Den lyckliga demokratin*. Ny, utökad upplaga. Stockholm: Bokförlaget Pan/Norstedts, 1967.

www.ingramcontent.com/pod-product-compliance
Lightning Source LLC
Chambersburg PA
CBHW070913160426
43193CB00011B/1443